I'd Rather Have A Root Canal
Than Do Cold Calling!

I'd Rather Have A Root Canal
Than Do Cold Calling!

Shawn A. Greene

SuccessWorks Publishing
San Pablo, California

I'D RATHER HAVE A ROOT CANAL
THAN DO COLD CALLING!

Many of the quotations shown in this book are drawn from:
"The 2,548 Best Things Ever Said," Robert Byrne, Galahad Books.
And "The Concise Columbia Dictionary of Quotations,"
Robert Andrews, Columbia Books.

This book is dedicated
with a tiny smirk
to all the guys who
were surprised I could,

and
with great love to JD,
the guy who
always believes
I can.

"I'd Rather Have a Root Canal!"

I was about to deliver my first class in telemarketing. The participants slowly trickled in, grabbing a croissant and coffee before sitting down.

I noticed their faces were sullen and almost everyone who was not eating sat with their arms crossed. Worst of all, only a few caught my eye and returned my smile.

This may have been my first telemarketing class, but it certainly wasn't the first time I needed to find out what was going on—and fast! I abandoned the warm and fuzzy icebreaker I'd planned and asked the group to tell me how they felt about being in the telemarketing class.

The first student said, "My boss made me come."

The second said, "It's my job, whether I want to or not."

The third person said, "You wanna know how I feel about doing telemarketing? I'd rather have a root canal!"

More than ten years later, I have yet to hear a better description of how most people feel about telemarketing.

This Book

There are lots of books out there about telemarketing. What makes this one special is our consultative approach to telemarketing—and our approach to teaching you how to do it.

We know that your success requires more than a nifty script. You need the right expectations. You need tools to manage your telemarketing program. Most of all, you need to prevent frustration! This book walks you through learning all of this.

The Root Canal Effect

First on the list of becoming a successful telemarketer is changing your attitude.

Our aversion to *being* telemarketers comes from our dislike of the telemarketing calls we receive at home. Before you can turn this dislike over, you have to know where it comes from.

There was a time when phone calls were special events, especially long distance calls. Now, however, many calls are an interruption of precious personal time. This slops over into the business context.

Our dislike of these calls certainly has something to do with the fact they often come at a bad time. However, what we hate most about these calls is based on what the caller says and does, not the call itself. The calls we hate to receive are disrespectful, invasive, and canned.

"I'm not confused, I'm just well mixed."

Robert Frost, poet and one of the first spin doctors.

We Hear Ya, Mr. Dangerfield!

All of us prefer to be treated as important individuals. We want our opinions, wants, desires, needs and preferences respected. And, we want to be asked about those opinions, wants, desires, needs and preferences.

Callers that don't try to find out if we have need or interest in what they're selling demonstrate a lack of respect for us as individuals. The same goes for fundraising calls. When the caller doesn't ask if we have an interest in the charity or issue, we feel pushed.

> We don't want to be like those guys who pester us at home!

Callers who don't get right to the point show us they have little respect for our time or intelligence. We know this is a sales call: What are you selling?

Some of the other ways callers create a feeling of disrespect include:

- Blithely dismissing our objections with a rote, "I understand..."

- Ignoring obvious signs this is *not* a good time to talk on the phone.

- Sounding as if they are doing us a favor, "I'm calling to save you money on..."

All of the above behaviors are called an "assumptive approach." These callers assume we want what they are selling. Whether or not this approach ever really worked in the past, it certainly doesn't work now. When we are pushed, we usually push back!

In addition, very few people want to <u>make</u> these types of calls. Who wants to act that way, right?

The Invasion of the Giant Telemarketers

The calls we hate to receive are also invasive. When we feel invaded—just a little bit in danger—we go on the defensive.

Many of us raise our defenses as soon as we realize a telemarketer is on the other end of the line; usually, right after that long auto-dialer pause.

Our discomfort escalates as the telemarketer starts in with seemingly innocuous questions, such as "Is this Mrs. Greene?" and "How are you?"

The questions feel overly personal and out of context. Sometimes, we worry that when we confirm something as simple as our name, we open ourselves to the danger of fraud. We also sense this line of questioning is a ploy to get us saying "yes" so often that we say yes to whatever they are selling. (We are right.)

To combat this feeling of invasion, we become more and more defensive. We may stay on the line, but we're less and less open to what the telemarketer is saying.

This old, manipulative style is very counter-productive. Telemarketers who use this style have to work very hard for a sale because we have trouble letting go of our defenses: We have more objections. We take longer to decide. We say "no" more often. We also cancel more often.

Is This Flounder Fresh?

In addition to the assumptive, invasive telemarketing approach, the whole canned thing falls flat. Although, if we didn't have to put up with the rest of it, we'd probably have more fun with canned part.

Who writes these things?

Our training workshop participants have great stories about how they befuddled a caller stuck in canned-script-land.

One woman tells long distance service telemarketers, "I don't have a phone."

A fellow with a very deep voice tells them he's not old enough to talk to them on the phone.

Amazingly, most callers go right into their scripted objection-handler without even a chuckle!

My own recent favorite follows. Keep in mind my name is Shawn, I'm female, and not married to a guy named Greene:

"Hello, may I speak to Mr. Greene?"
"No."
"Shawn Greene?"
"Yes."
"Mrs. Greene?"
"No."
"Mrs. Shawn Greene?"
(Taking pity on the poor thing) "I'm Shawn Greene."
"Mrs. Greene, how are you? I'm calling..."

That caller lost me as soon as I lost interest in teasing him.

When telemarketers use scripts written by other people, they don't sound real. When someone doesn't sound real, our defenses go up.

The Whole Sorry Story

This is a pretty sad state of affairs! Telemarketers who assume we want what they're selling; who try to push us into saying yes so often that we're ready to buy the Brooklyn Bridge; and who don't even sound like human beings.

No wonder we have "call reluctance." We don't want to be like those pesty telemarketers. Our prospects won't like it either. This all adds up to failure.

So Why Telemarket?

With all the antipathy toward telemarketers, why bother? Here's why:

☎ Efficacy and low cost:

The telephone gives the most bang for the buck. On average, telemarketers reach 33 live people out of 100 calls.

Compare that to direct mail (average 1%) or even networking (how many people can you meet at one event?).

☎ It's easy to use:

A telephone is standard equipment. Unlike writing great direct mail or designing a radio ad, there are no special skills or experience required to make a phone call.

☎ You can stand out:

The final reason to use telemarketing is because you can be a star! At this time, most telemarketers still make calls we hate to receive. Think about the results you'll generate when you make phone calls that are truly different. That's what this book is all about.

Turning Your Attitude Around

Turning your attitude around is simple: Make calls you'd like to receive!

Make calls that are the opposite of the calls we find so annoying. You want to make calls that are:

☎ Direct and up-front.
☎ Respectful.
☎ In your own words.

> Make calls you'd
> like to receive!

These telemarketing calls are very successful and you won't mind making them nearly as much.

The Bad News ~ A Learning Curve

Now that you know what creates call reluctance, you may think turning it around will be easy. Well, with practice, it is indeed easy to generate success. However, there is a learning curve.

For some reason, new telemarketers tend to emulate the very calls they dislike. Maybe they do this because they've grown so accustomed to pushy, canned calls that it's the model that jumps to mind.

As you learn to make consultative telemarketing calls, you must also un-learn the old pushy style. You'll have to focus, practice, and persist to accomplish this.

We don't want you to think telemarketing is always fun once you've learned it, either. There will be plenty of days when you get great results and have a fabulous time talking to neat people. Unfortunately, there will be plenty of, er…other days.

Not to worry, though! We'll give you tools to make sure you have way more fun and successful days than not.

"I'm extraordinarily patient
provided I get my own way in the end."

Margaret Thatcher, former British Prime Minister
and probably a very bossy older sister.

Great Expectations

As we mentioned, making good calls is only part of story. To have the greatest success you also have to know when to use telemarketing and what to expect.

One of the main reasons telemarketing fails is because people get frustrated. The reason they get frustrated is their expectations are out of whack. This section focuses on the right expectations.

"I like criticism, but it must be my way."

Mark Twain, who may have bonded well with Ms. Thatcher.

It's Not Really "Sales and Marketing"

The right expectations starts with defining what you're doing. Though lots of people use the word "marketing" as a euphemism for "selling," marketing and selling are really two different things.

 Marketing is whatever you do to gain the favorable attention of prospects, and regain the attention of customers. Selling is what happens once you have their attention.

We should really say "marketing and sales" because marketing comes first.

The Big Picture

It helps to have a model of the marketing and selling process. Here's what the whole process looks like:

Marketing brings prospects into the process.

Once you connect with a prospect, you leave marketing and start selling.

Selling includes qualifying (evaluating business fit), presenting that fit, and asking for the business.

The selling process "ends" when you open a new business relationship. From there, you move on to account management.

You can do all of this on the phone—but should you?

Reality Check

It is possible to market <u>and</u> sell over the phone. That's right, lots of people can run through the entire marketing and sales process over the phone, without ever meeting prospects and customers face-to-face.

Is it *prospecting*? Yup, telemarketing is prospecting on the phone.

It's also possible that you can succeed in marketing and selling over the phone in one, single, stand-alone phone call.

On the other hand, expecting to succeed in marketing *and* selling over the phone may be setting yourself up for failure. As we said before, having strange expectations only creates frustration.

The reality of your marketplace drives your ability to succeed in marketing and selling on the phone. So, you need to figure out your "reality."

We've provided you with two ways to figure out whether you should expect to market and sell over the phone, or just market. There's a quick and easy Reality Check on the next page. A more detailed presentation of the issues follows.

Reality Check ~ The Short Version

Mark any of these statements that apply:

____   I usually know my prospects' name and how to reach them.

____   I sell something that is very familiar to most people.

____   Most of my prospects don't require a proposal.

____   Most of my prospects don't want to see any materials.

____   I usually close the deal in one conversation.

____   I feel very comfortable on the phone.

If you marked most or all of the items listed, it makes sense for you to expect to market <u>and</u> sell over the phone. So, go for it! Just make sure you read this whole book before you get started.

If you didn't mark all or most of the items listed, then you should market on the phone—and sell in person. We'll tell you how to move from marketing to asking for a sales appointment, not to worry.

If you're not sure (after all, how many is "most"?), read over the long version of the Reality Check.

Reality Check ~ The Long Version

To figure out if you should market and sell on the phone, or just market, consider these issues:

- **Simplicity and familiarity.**

If you're selling something which is rather simple and very familiar to prospects, then you can probably sell over the phone. Chances are also good you can complete the deal in one phone call.

For example, if you are marketing things or services such as…

- Office delivery services.
- Long-distance services.
- Small donations for charity….

Then chances are darn good you can market and sell in on the phone, and in one phone call.

On the other hand, if you're selling something that is simple but <u>unfamiliar</u>, you probably won't be able to complete the entire sale over the phone.

For example, when alternate long distance services were first available, prospects were not willing to buy until they met the salesperson face-to-face. The reason has to do with the second issue: trust.

- **Level of trust required.**

Think about all the types of services we might research (shop for) on the phone, but would not consider buying without having first met the person. Dentists, doctors, house-cleaners and daycare providers are just a few from this list. These services require a high measure of personal trust.

A high measure of trust must also be present when buying something unfamiliar. Regardless of your product or service, when selling to prospects who have not purchased such an item or service before, you may find you must meet them in person to conduct the sale.

> Look me in the eye and make that promise, why don't cha?

Now, mind you, *your* familiarity with what you're selling doesn't count. It's your prospects perspective that counts here.

- **Commitment required.**

Buying always involves a leap of faith; how big a leap often depends on the above issue. When we can't see the person we're buying from, the leap gets a little wider.

When we have to pay for something before receiving it and/or make a long term commitment, the leap is always wider.

Likewise, if your customers have to commit to giving you something really personal—like their money—trust is an issue. This is especially true when you're marketing for an unknown company.

Things that require a huge commitment should come with an escape hatch. There has to be a way buyers can get their money back (e.g., by paying with credit card), or some sort of grace period before the full commitment kicks in.

If you can't do this and your product or service requires a big commitment, you should telemarket, but sell in person.

The same goes for selling for an outfit that doesn't carry instant trustworthiness. Market on the phone and sell in person.

- **Last, but not least, how you feel.**

You can overcome many of the above challenges without working in-person with your prospects. You can:

- Provide written information and other visual materials (e.g. flow charts, pictures, or website) to discuss over the phone.

- Provide referrals, so prospects can talk with someone other than the salesperson before deciding to buy.

- Provide a money-back guarantee, or provide the product or service before invoicing.

However, none of the above methods can overcome your own reluctance. If you don't feel confident in telemarketing, you'll need some time to see that it works.

Your confidence will grow as you practice using the phone in a consultative style. We promise. This means you may indeed be able to market and sell over the phone, which widens your marketplace considerably and saves you all that time stuck in traffic! In the meantime, stick with telemarketing and leave selling for in-person.

Back at the Ranch: Marketing or Selling?

If the reality check indicates you'll just market, so be it. If you will market and sell, we have some sage advice for you: Take it one step at a time. Look to succeed first with marketing. Look to succeed with selling second.

Since you'll be starting with marketing, it's time to get a fix on what telemarketing "success" looks like.

Success by the Numbers

Marketing includes things like:

- Networking
- Advertising
- Direct and email
- Internet
- ☎ Telemarketing

Most forms of marketing have been around so long that expectations can be expressed in the form of mathematical equations.

🖃 For example, we know the average rate of response for direct mail is about 1%. So if you want at least 10 responses, you'd have to mail…let me get out the calculator here…at least 1,000 pieces. Wow!

Shades of story problems, Batman!

🖥 The rate of return for email used to be about 1%, but it's gone way down from that.

☽ Telemarketing's rate of return is much better. And we're not saying that just because we wrote a book about it. Flip open almost any book about marketing and you'll see the figures we show you on the next page…

☞ On average, this is what you can expect from telemarketing:

☎ Out of 100 phone calls, using a *freezing* cold list, you will connect with 33 live humans.

☎ Of those 33 live humans, 11 will choose to talk with you <u>and</u> have a good fit with what you're marketing and selling.

☎ Of those 11, to whom you make a presentation, 4 or 5 will say yes.

That's a total return of 4% to 5%. And, when making warmer calls—using a more specific and better-qualified list—your return will be even higher.

Keep Your Eye on the Prize

Since we're talking marketing here—not selling—there are really only two benchmarks of success to keep in mind:

- Using an average, telemarketing brings at least 33 of 100 prospects into the selling process.

- And, of those 33 prospects, an average of 11 choose to talk with you <u>and</u> have a fit with what you're marketing and selling.

The above is the description of success for telemarketing.

The above also describes what you can expect to have happen. If your averages don't live up to those figures, then something is wrong. You should check the troubleshooting section to get some help.

When Telemarketing *Rules*

Telemarketing is just one form of marketing, so it will probably fill a different spot in your marketing plan, at different times. Keep the following points in mind as you determine where it fits. (Be sure to re-evaluate your plan at least twice a year.)

Telemarketing should have the lead in your marketing plan:

- **When your business is new:**

   For many businesses (e.g. consultants), networking is the most effective marketing method. But networking takes one to two *years* to begin to roll.

   There are also lots of businesses that thrive on word of mouth. That, too, takes time to get rolling.

   In the meantime, pick up that phone!

- **When your prospects don't hang out much at networking events.**

   An awful lot of businesses actually rely on a sort of second-tier networking. You don't meet your prospects directly at networking events. Instead, you meet people, who meet or know your prospects, and those people give you leads. The fancy term for this is "referral."

   If your prospects don't hang out at networking events at all—if your networking is mostly second-tier—then it can take even longer for results. So, in the meantime…you guessed it…pick up the phone!

- **When you don't have the resources to use direct mail or the internet effectively.**

  We're talking money here. If you don't have enough money to make direct mail and/or the internet work well enough…pick up the phone! It's easy to set up good cold calling and you get a lot of bang for that buck.

  Here's a hot tip for those sole proprietors out there: Get a cold calling buddy and call for each other. If you have someone else cold calling for you, your business appears "bigger" than it is. Plus, it's often easier to cold-call for someone else.

- **When you want to develop a business relationship, rather than sell just one time to each customer.**

  Calling someone on the phone lends a very personal touch. Obviously, if you want an on-going relationship with your customers, that personal touch is important.

  Sure, flowers are cool, but what would Mom say if you didn't call her?

- **When you're building your marketing lists.**

  You can create your own marketing lists, instead of buying them. And, even if you buy a list, you'll have to keep the list up-to-date.

  Before you send something in the mail, if that's what you choose to do, you better call to make sure you have the right name and address.

- **When you need to take action <u>now</u>.**

  Whenever you're champing at the bit and feeling like you can't wait any longer, whenever you're stressed about not enough new business, then telemarket!

Now we'll describe how to use this information to prevent a strong desire to throw your phone out of the window in frustration.

Who's in Charge Here?

An amazing amount of frustration comes from weird ideas about what you can, or should be able to, control.

You might not be conscious of these strange ideas floating around in your head. In fact, if we were to ask you about control from the *customer's* side of the story, you'd say that you not only don't want to be controlled or manipulated, it's impossible for people to do that. But, for some reason, put a marketing or sales hat on ya and you act like your job is to control the world (but in a nice way, of course).

How do we know this goes on? We see it surface in the words clients use to describe the marketing and sales process. We hear it in their voices as they describe what they think they "should" be doing. And we see these weird ideas about control undermine people's success—until we set them straight!

"There is no human problem which could not be solved, if people would simply do as I advise."

Gore Vidal, famous author and control freak.

A Primer on "Control"

I will now share with you some great truths about cold calling and selling. After reading this part, you will be completely calm and sure of yourself. It will be as if I have waved a magic wand over you and you will never again experience doubt or frustration.

Ha! Here's what you should do: Tag this part. Bookmark it (the old kind). Then, when you start feeling frustrated or ineffective, read this part again. Keep reading it until its wisdom sinks in.

☹ There is no such thing as a "great" telemarketing list with completely accurate information. People move around too much these days. Heck, area codes change almost weekly!

Therefore, you are not in control of finding this fabulous list and buying it. You cannot succeed at creating or buying a "great" telemarketing list.

☺ You can find and buy really good lists when you know what to expect. And you can certainly control management of an ever-changing telemarketing list. We'll tell you how in the scripting section.

☹ You cannot make people pick up the phone.

Some people think there are tricks for calling people and magically causing them to be there and/or pick up the phone. Calling really early and really late are two of these supposed tricks of the trade.

It's true that calling early and late might get you in contact with people you've had trouble reaching before. However, it's a BIG mistake to set your sights on the number of people you actually reach on the phone.

Focus on what you can control. In this case, all you control is dialing the number. (More about this, later.)

☺ And, you can increase your chances of calling the right person at the right time by telemarketing consistently. Luck does play a part—call more often and you're more likely to get lucky!

☹ You can't make people call you back.

This might be news for you: Your cold calling success does not rely on getting people to call you back. Thank goodness! Because most people will not call you back. That's normal.

☺ You can get more people to call you back by leaving a fabulous marketing voicemail. We'll tell you how to do this.

☹ You can't make someone talk with you.

There are really, truly no magic words or tricks of language that somehow change someone's mind, manipulate them and make them want to talk with you. (Ask yourself: can you be manipulated that way?)

> At this stage, someone who won't talk with you is not a challenge—they're not a prospect!

☺ You can give it your best shot and let go before you make a bad impression.

You're about to learn how to make a very effective cold call. Still, when you're cold-calling, you don't want to try too darn hard to overcome objections. Most of the time, especially if you're a beginner, it's best to let go and dial the next number.

☹ You can't make someone want or need or have in interest in what you're selling.

Your opinions on a prospect's needs, wants, or interests don't count. Again, you cannot manipulate people into suddenly wanting what you're selling. For example, you cannot "create" a sense of urgency.

> If they don't see a need, that need doesn't exist.

A real prospect sees a need, wants to fix a problem, or has an interest.

☺ You can catch prospects' interest (we'll tell you how). You can also uncover needs, wants, and a sense of urgency.

You can qualify prospects so you don't waste your time and energy.

And, you can heighten someone's desire for what you're selling—but this doesn't happen while you're *marketing*! To increase someone's desire or interest in what you're selling, you need to be deeper into a conversation.

Making it Stick

It's one thing to hear (or read) about what you can control, it's another thing to actually focus on what you control. Here's how to make this information work for you on a day-to-day basis.

☎ Set numeric "dials" goals.

You can't control having the correct phone number, reaching the right person, or reaching a person at all. So don't set telemarketing goals based on those things!

The number of conversations (sales calls), or the number of new business accounts (closed deals) is definitely jumping the gun. So don't use those to set telemarketing goals, either.

There is really only one thing you can control in telemarketing: Making the call.

To make this sink in and work for you, set a goal for the number of calls you'll make: period. We call these "dials" goals. (If you were born after the invention of push button phones, humor us.)

☎ Set and take rewards.

Learning to telemarket is about changing behaviors and attitudes. You're gutting it through feeling uncomfortable. You're actually building new neural pathways in your brain. This is hard work!

Even after you've learned how to telemarket and experienced the pleasures of success, telemarketing will still sometimes be hard work.

We humans don't do much without some reward. Face it, most of us wouldn't brush our teeth even once a week if toothpaste didn't taste pretty good and leave us all the more kissable.

To make sure you reap the rewards of telemarketing, you have to give yourself a reason to do it. Closed sales won't be enough motivation because that's too far down the road. You need something immediate and something you get <u>every</u> time you telemarket. You need rewards.

We recommend rewards that take about ten minutes to enjoy.
For example:

- Have a snack.
- Call a friend.
- Take a walk around the block.
- Watch the soaps for ten minutes.
- Play a computer game.

Objectives According to Spock

Preventing frustration is also about having objectives that make sense for marketing. We want to cover this along with the funnel, so we've got to skip to the next page…

When you are telemarketing, you are moving through the first step: marketing. If you try to hurry the marketing and sales process, the only thing you'll succeed in doing is driving yourself crazy.

So, in addition to setting dials goals, you want to be sure your telemarketing objectives make sense.

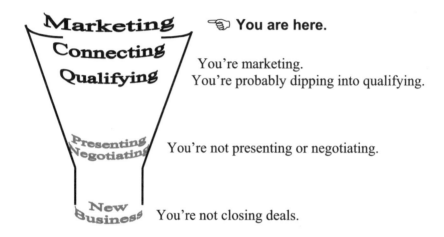

Marketing ☞ **You are here.**

Connecting

Qualifying You're marketing.
You're probably dipping into qualifying.

Presenting
Negotiating You're not presenting or negotiating.

New
Business You're not closing deals.

Some of our clients post a copy of this funnel where they can see it while telemarketing. Posting a picture isn't enough, though. You have to match your telemarketing objectives with reasonable, logical expectations for results.

One of the best ways to do this is use appropriate language to describe your objectives.

Using the right words programs the right logic process, which in turn programs your attitude.

> Train your brain: Use words that match reality. You can't *get* appointments—you can *request* them.

Your Mission, Should You Wish to Actually Succeed

Here's a list of the best telemarketing objectives:

☎ Explore: Locate contacts and find out how to reach them.

☎ Treasure hunt: Ask existing contacts for leads or referrals.

☎ Request an exchange of information: Do some early qualifying.

☎ Request an appointment: Ask for a phone or in-person sales meeting.

☎ Hey there: Give a "heads up" about materials you're sending, or have just recently sent.

☎ No time marketing: Call before or after hours and leave voicemails.

More on Success and Sanity

Here's what you know so far about preventing frustration:

- Set numeric goals to focus on what you can control and where you are in the process.
- Use reasonable objectives and words that reflect reality.
- Set <u>and take</u> rewards to help make sure you stick to it.

Here's a few more things you can do to prevent frustration:

- **Use a tracking sheet.** (Sample at the back of the book.)

The figures describing success are averages for all types of businesses. Your averages may be different. Track your telemarketing over several months, then use the data to calculate your averages.

If your average results are better than what is shown—cool! You can either make fewer dials or reap the rewards of more business.

If your average results are not at least at par, then you may need some help. See the troubleshooting section.

- **Mark off your calls as you make them, one by one.** (Use the tracking sheet or make one of your own.)

Telemarketing is the very first step for what can be a l o o o n g process. With each call you make, you are making progress, but there may be days when it doesn't seem like you're getting anywhere.

The physical act of marking off calls reminds you that you are indeed making progress.

- **Clear your calling space.**

Avoid distractions by clearing off your desk before you start telemarketing. All you should have is the list (or computer, if using call management software), your scripts, scratch paper, something to drink, and the phone.

When to Let Go

We teach that you need Persistence, Integrity, Guts® to succeed in telemarketing. Persistence can easily become pestering—which will bug both you and your prospects—so you need some advice on when to let go.

Let's start with voicemail. Out of 90 cold call dials, you'll reach about 30 live humans. That means 60 calls will end up as wrong numbers, disconnected numbers, a few people who won't talk to you at all, and lots and lots of voicemail.

When you get voicemail, rejoice and leave a great message!

Voicemail is the coolest marketing tool since the telephone was invented. However, you don't want to waste your time or make a bad impression by pestering.

☎ **Call three times.** If you don't reach the person on the third call, let them know you're going to slow down subsequent calls in your message.

Put these contacts on a back burner and call less often, though still consistently.

You will also encounter a few prospects who tell you to call back; which you should do. How often? Call again three times. If you get the prospect on the phone and they say call back again, find out what's going on.

But, are they just trying to put you off? Here's one way to uncover the real story…

"I wonder if what you're really trying to tell me is thanks, but no thanks?"

This usually prompts them to come clean.

Now, if they say they really don't want/need/whatever what you're offering, then you have a decision to make. Put this prospect aside completely, forever and ever? Or try them again later?

In case you're wondering…we vote you try them again later.

But…

You might be thinking this is a pretty whimpy way to cold call. What happened to persisting? What happened to overcoming their objections? Well, it's time for another reality check…

a) If you're already having trouble cold-calling, trying to overcome objections raises the bar way too high. You won't succeed as much and you'll get frustrated. So why go there? Just move on to the next call.

b) The person who presents an objection in a marketing conversation—especially if they bring it up right off the bat—is probably not going to listen to reason.

   Most often, you'll give your best objection-handler, they will counter, you'll give your next objection-handler…and before you know it you've spent five minutes chasing after a lost cause.

Someone who won't talk with you is not a "challenge," he or she is not a prospect. Let go for now.

Let The Prospect Play, too!

There will be lots of situations in which some sort of follow-up seems to be the right thing to do.

For example, let's say the prospect tells you, "We're not in the market for automatic brooms just now."

Here's how you should handle it, and why:

- **Ask the prospect if you can follow up.**

  "May I contact you again?"

- If the answer is yes, **ask the prospect to tell you HOW** you should follow up—don't tell them what you'll do.

  "How would you like me to follow up; phone, email, or mail?"

  Their answer tells you a little more about this prospect's preferred modus operandi.

- Then, **ask** the prospect to **tell you WHEN** you should follow up.

  "When should I contact you again?"

  This gives the prospect a chance to have even more input, which helps develop more of a real relationship between you two.

- After the prospect tells you when, **ask WHY** at that time?

  "Okay, I'll email you in a few weeks. Any particular reason why a few weeks?"

  This question uncovers all kinds of information goodies; from, I just don't want to think about this now, to we have a new boss, to I'm going on vacation, to we will be interested in buying this sort of thing in a few weeks.

It takes guts to ask questions like the ones above. Take heart, take a chance and you'll reap the rewards.

☞ What should you do if they say, "I'll call you."? First of all, translate that to, "I don't have the guts to say no." And then tell them,

"Okay. And if I don't hear from you in a couple weeks or so, I'll give you a call."

Do call back. Just don't get too excited about this prospect.

You've now learned what you need to know for setting the right expectations and preventing frustration. Well done! See the next page for a handy summary.

Here's What You Know so Far

☎ The way to overcome your dislike of telemarketing is to make calls you'd like to receive.

These calls are direct and up-front, respect each prospect's unique needs and interests, and are in your own words. (How to do this is covered in the next section.)

☎ One key to preventing frustration is to know what to expect and what constitutes success. Expectations for success, on average:

- Of 100 dials, you'll reach 33 live humans.
- Of those 33 people, 11 conversations will generate a presentation.
- Of those 11 presentations, you'll have 3 or 4 units of new business.

Your numbers will probably be better than these. If they aren't, see the troubleshooting section.

☎ Another key to preventing frustration is focusing on where you are in the process: At the top of the funnel—marketing.

Using dials goals and rewards will give you the right focus.

☎ Luck *is* a factor! Telemarket consistently to give yourself the best chance of talking to the right person, at the right time.

☎ Try three times, then put them on a back burner. Keep calling, just not as often.

"If I had my life to live over,
I'd make the same mistakes, only sooner."

Tallulah Bankhead, famous for her wit and ability to drink other wits under the table.

Scripting ~ The Inside Scoop

Attention, Skipper-aheaders:

Successful consultative telemarketing requires more than making great phone calls.

To succeed, you need the right expectations. Most of all, you need to prevent frustration. The first half of this book walked you through learning all of that. If you skipped over that section—well, who are we to try and boss you around? Still, we encourage you to read the first section before you start this one.

In this section, we'll tell you why scripting your calls is important, how to create effective scripts, and how to make your scripts sound just like you—no cans involved.

"Why don't you write books people can read?"

Nora Joyce to her husband, James, who apparently did not take her advice.

What Works: Calls You'd Like to Receive

Hark back to the reason we don't like to telemarket: We don't want to <u>be</u> like the telemarketers who bother us at home.

It's not really the calls themselves that bug us. What bothers us is that so many of these calls are disrespectful, invasive, and canned. So, in order to succeed, we want to make calls that are the opposite.

We want to make calls that are:

☎ Direct and up-front about the reason for the call.

☎ Respectful of each individual's needs and interests.

☎ In our own words.

Before we launch you into drafting scripts, you need to know a little about what's going on behind the scenes in communication.

Wave, if You Can See Me

Think of communication as having three elements: The words themselves, tone of voice, and body language.

A good deal of communication comes through body language. This includes all kinds of physical attributes; from a smile (we can tell a real one from a fake one), to gestures, to our whole body posture.

We're born ready to send and receive lots of body language. People who don't even speak the same language can communicate using body language. For example, shaking a fist means pretty much the same thing all over the planet.

However, lots of body language is learned. For example, in some parts of the world, showing your teeth when you smile isn't considered polite and kids learn that very early.

When on the phone, callers send almost as much body language as they do in person. The trouble is, the person at the other end of the line can't see them. To compensate, listeners pick up on the other elements of communication. Therefore, your tone of voice and words are extremely important.

> On the phone, tone is almost everything.

It's *How* You Say it

Lots of new telemarketers worry about sounding nervous. The good news is listeners hardly ever pick up on nervousness. (In addition, the work you're about to do on scripting will reduce nervousness.)

What comes through the loudest on the phone is any sort of disconnect between what the caller <u>says</u> and what the caller really <u>means</u>. Listeners are hyper-sensitive to hidden agendas—even benign secret agendas.

In addition, most of us are not great liars. When we say something we don't quite mean, listeners can tell. That is, that's true for most of us. There are some people who lie very effectively. They're called con artists.

☎ **Be up-front about the real reason for your call.**

No, Wait, it's *What* You Say

Okay, so when we don't say what we really mean, listeners can tell and they don't like it. But, wait, there's more.

Most of us aren't great actors, either. When we use words that don't match our natural everyday style of talking, listeners don't like that either. Our tone seems off.

Using someone else's words causes a disconnect. Listeners' survival instincts perk up because they sense something is not quite right. When our survival instincts engage, so do our defenses.

☎ **Use your own words.** You'll feel more comfortable and you'll sound better.

And Now, on Center Stage

Having just said that most of us are not great liars or actors, I now take some of that back.

"Liar" is far too strong a word for it. However, most of us are fairly good fibbers. We can smoothly decline a second helping of lima beans because we, um…want to save room for dessert.

We have easy access to a range of words and tone that we use across a variety of situations, in a variety of roles.

We use different words when we're sharing a couple beers with friends than we do when chatting it up with our boss. We use sports lingo with ease, and we can give pretty convincing performances of "The Three Little Pigs" when we want to.

We're born with this ability to act—to manage how we communicate. As we grow up we get even better at it because we practice communicating in different ways. We learn to take clues from situations and the people around us to communicate appropriately.

When we get lots of practice in many different situations, we become very adept communicators. We also become comfortable in a wider and wider range of situations.

You can use your innate ability to manage how you communicate to make great calls. We'll help this along by going over the key elements of successful, consultative calls and give you practice in scripting.

The Elements Of Successful Consultative Scripts

☎ When calling Gatekeepers:

Who you are.
Why you're calling.
Ask for help and/or request to proceed.
Description of likely contacts, just in case.
Thank you.

☎ When calling contacts/prospects:

Who you are.
Ad (optional).
Why you're calling.
Request to proceed.
Information sharing, including qualifying prospects.
Check-in, or request to go to next step.

☎ Voicemail:

Who you are.
Ad.
Why you're calling.
Call to action.
Your next step.
Who you are again, and how to reach you.

Go With the Flow

Your calls aren't necessarily going to follow the above flow every time.
Scripting each element helps you pick and choose what's appropriate, when.

We'll start by scripting how you'll say who you are.

Who I am? Jeez!

You might think that covering the first element—who you are—is silly. Not so, grasshopper!

For example, my full name is Shawn Greene. People often hear that as "Charlene" and "Maureen."

What's worse, they sometimes get stuck hearing a name that doesn't make sense to them right away. "What did you say your name is?" they inquire, their irritation and distrust growing already.

☎ You might not want to use your full name. Try it both ways. If people don't hear you clearly, then make a change.

Who you are is also about your organization: Who you represent. Saying the business name might need a little work, too.

For example, one client, calling from "Irminghouse Labels," kept being heard as calling from "Mickey Mouse Labels." This was not the impression he wanted to make! Once he started saying things like, "I'm calling from a label-making company," he got far better results.

What's in a name?

In addition, the business name may not be enough by itself, even when it's easily understood. You might need a short explanation.

If the business name comes along with enough context for most listeners, you probably don't need to tack on an explanation. For example, if you're calling from "Disneyland Travel Services," you probably don't need to say any more.

On the other hand, if you're calling from JP Associates, there's no context for most listeners. What does JP Associates do? Why is JP Associates calling us? What's going on? Alarm, alarm!

To prevent defensiveness, you have to provide that context. For example, "I'm calling from JP Associates, an executive search firm."

☎ If your business name isn't well-known or doesn't indicate context, include a brief description or identity-statement.

There's one last bit of advice about saying who you are: You're not who you're with.

Do not say things like, "My name is Alice from JP Associates."

Your name is Alice. You're calling from JP Associates, an executive search firm.

Why You're Calling

Of all the elements of great consultative calls, people have the most trouble with the "why" part. We stumble over being direct and up-front about the reason for the call. We have trouble with this for two reasons.

"That's *interesting*" he said, and I knew I was sunk.

The first reason is because we have way more experience with *in*direct. Here in the United States, it's common practice to use obtuse language in marketing and sales. We're surrounded by this sort of language from a very early age.

For an example in contrast, consider ads for deodorants. Ads usually only hint deodorants are meant to keep us from smelling bad. The language has gotten a little more direct over time, but certainly not as direct as a new ad running on ESPN. The ad is for men's deodorant. The voiceover states the deodorant, "…gets rid of that really stinking sweat."

Well. My goodness. That certainly says what it means. Of course, being *that* direct may offend too many prospects, so you probably shouldn't use that ad as a model.

The other reason we have trouble being direct and up-front about the reason for our call is that it's just plain scary.

Most people would rather avoid rejection, confrontation, or disputes. Indirect language helps us do this. By using fuzzy language, we're not hanging out there with our intentions clearly blowing in the wind.

Persistence, Integrity, Guts®

Savage and Greene captures the essence of successful marketing and selling with the acronym PIG. When it comes to consultative telemarketing, you'll need persistence and you'll definitely have to show some guts. You'll simply have to ignore the little measure of fear and make the calls anyway.

You'll also have to apply integrity. In this case, integrity means being true to your real objective for each call.

We can help you be true to your real objectives. We'll start by illustrating what not to say.

Please, Do Not Attempt This Yourself

Here are some examples of what not to say, and why. These are all real calls!

Some callers try to drop names…

"Mr. McGillicudy is expecting my call. Please put me through."

Well, that name is a fake one I use when I fill out raffle forms, and our receptionist knows it. Plus, even if there was a McGillicudy in our office, he'd want a reminder about the reason for the call—it's the polite thing to do!

Some callers seem to be desperately seeking decisiveness...

"May I speak to person who makes decisions about your long distance services?

This wouldn't be such a bad approach, except it doesn't even acknowledge the fact a human has answered the phone—a human who may even make those decisions. Why don't they just ask, "May I speak to your Mommy, please?"

Some callers are apparently interested in our thought process...

"I'm calling to ask if you've thought about how adding double-paned windows would add value to your home."

O, puleeze! We know they aren't just calling to run a survey. Plus, answering this question with an affirmative is too close to making a commitment to buy.

Some telemarketers fancy themselves as educators...

"I'm calling today to tell you about a terrific offer."

O gosh! Thank you for calling to tell us! Come on, already. We know this is a sales call. What are you selling?

Some telemarketers like to give us a test...

"Do you know that most of your credit cards probably charge you more than 18%?"

Are they saying we're stupid? Are they trying to make us feel bad for paying such high rates? Plus, this telemarketer is in trouble if our interest rates are lower.

The secret ingrate calls a lot...

"We're just calling to thank you for your support over the past year..."

"Just"? Gee, we'd really like that, if only it were true!

The worst are the guys who call with a whip in their hand...

"We see that you haven't activated your new combination calling card and credit card, so I'm going to take care of that for you right now."

We'll really have to be rude to stop this guy, so we will be!

Familiarity Breeds Error

Unless you're one of those guys who hangs up on all telemarketers, you've heard versions of the preceding indirect styles many times.

You've heard them so many times that when you start to write your own scripts, your first instinct may be to copy them. In fact, we can almost bet on it because this happens so often in our workshops.

Remember, part of the work of learning consultative telemarketing involves unlearning the old approach. To help you unlearn the old approach and learn the new one, we'll analyze and translate the examples we showed you on the previous pages.

"Mr. McGillicudy is expecting my call. Please put me through."

This ineffective technique fails for two reasons:

One – it requires you to work up a really good case of fake bravado. You have to pretend you know this guy and that he is expecting your call. To carry this off, you'll have to be a very good fake.

You'll also have to be completely sure this is the right guy (and that he is a guy). If you're wrong, you're in big trouble!

Two – This technique fails because it is a technique. Everyone sees right through it. You will accomplish nothing more than making this gatekeeper mad at you.

This approach is so bad—it's such schmoozing—we're not even going to attempt to fix it.

"May I speak to the person who makes decisions about your long distance services?

The good news: The caller asks "May I?"

One problem is this call skips over the part where the caller asks who that great decision-maker is. Since the caller doesn't ask about that, the message is that the person on the other end of the line is a mere connector of calls. Who wants to be treated like that?

Plus, the person who picks up the phone may well be the person the caller is looking for. Treating him or her as a non-person is not a great start.

The telemarketer would like to (A) find out who the long-distance decider is and (B) talk to that person. The best thing to do is to tackle those two things separately. We'll tell you why later. So, sticking with the first issue…

"I am calling about a terrific long distance service and I'd like to see if our service would work for you. Would you help me with information about who makes decisions about your long distance?"

This caller tells the person who picks up the phone why she's calling, which gives a context for the call. The caller uses <u>non-assumptive</u> words.

The caller also asks for the gatekeeper's help. Most people who pick up phones are happy to help when you respect them. And, you really do need their help, so this is the honest thing to say!

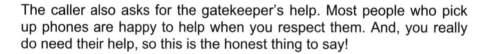

"I'm calling to ask if you've thought about how adding double-paned windows would add value to your home."

This caller is in trouble for about a zillion reasons. He's assuming way too much: That the listener is the homeowner; that he or she doesn't already have double-paned windows; and that he or she cares about adding value to their home.

His assumptive approach tries to jump over the part where he finds out if his double-paned windows are a fit with what each prospect wants or needs. This is bound to bug a lot of people.

Plus, the caller isn't really doing a survey to find out if people sit around <u>contemplating</u> their navel and double-paned windows. Listeners know this and therefore don't trust the telemarketer. Defenses go up instantly.

The telemarketer's objective is to perk prospects' attention. In the olden days, he could do this by saying something like, "Did you know you're losing hundreds of dollars through your windows?" These days, that sort of approach backfires. So, he should include an interest grabbing word or two—still directly stating the reason for his call.

"I'd like to tell you a bit about our energy-saving, double-paned windows and then see if you might be interested in discussing them with one of our sales reps."

Notice this example includes phrases such as, "I'd like to..." and "might be..." These phrases are far from assumptive, so prospects are more at ease.

These non-assumptive phrases are also based in reality. All the telemarketer can do is <u>ask</u>, so using these phrases helps prevent frustration for the telemarketer.

Double-paned windows aren't the sort of thing most people will buy on the phone. They probably want lots of information before making a commitment to poke holes in their walls. So the telemarketer keeps his focus on marketing and away from selling. Still, if all goes well, he intends to ask for a sales meeting. By saying that up-front, using "and then," he avoids the disconnect problem.

☎ However, you may notice the telemarketer doesn't say anything about qualifying the prospect. This is a choice you might have to make, too.

You might want to leave qualifying until the end of the conversation. This gives you a chance to develop prospects' interest first. On the other hand, you may develop interest only to find out you're not talking to a qualified prospect! We suggest you try both ways to see which works best. (See Just How Hot is That Prospect? section for more on qualifying.)

"I'm calling today to tell you about a terrific offer."

There are two big things wrong with this. First, we all know the telemarketer has way more on her mind than sharing information about an offer. Second, she doesn't say what the offer is for. Disconnect and distrust are on the rise!

"We have a terrific offer for subscriptions for The Chronicle. I'd like to tell you about the offer, and see if you might be interested in taking us up on it. Can I tell you about the offer?"

The key point in the first sentence is that the telemarketer identifies what the offer is for. This demonstrates respect for listeners.

The telemarketer has an easier job this way, too. If the prospect is going to say no (maybe they already get the Chronicle) it will probably come up now.

Notice the telemarketer <u>asks permission</u> to talk about the offer. She also states up-front that she'll want to know if the prospect wants to buy. That, too, is very good.

Sure, most people know the purchase is implied if the prospect likes the special offer. The point is to avoid mere implication. The more up-front you are, the more you demonstrate respect for the prospect.

"Do you know that most of your credit cards probably charge you more than 18%?"

My, my, my. Can you name all the things wrong with this? The telemarketer assumes the listener uses credit cards; that the interest rates are over 18%; and that the listener cares about the rates being over 18%.

In addition, this telemarketer sort of says that prospects are stupid if they don't know that and/or if they have cards with higher rates.

Finally, we know the telemarketer is not simply calling to give us a little test on our knowledge about interest rates. Disconnect, again.

"I'm calling from Big Bank. We offer credit cards that have interest rates below 18%. I'd like to find out if you might like to apply for one of our cards."

This script identifies the product brand (Big Bank); what's special about the brand; and makes a direct request for a sale.

Since credit cards are a very familiar product, but one that requires an application process, it makes sense to go right to asking for an agreement to buy/apply.

Notice that even this very direct approach uses <u>non-assumptive</u>, soft-sell words.

"We're just calling to thank you for your support over the past year."

This is a fund-raising call. They probably are indeed grateful for the last donation; however, in this example the word "just" means "only." They are definitely not <u>only</u> calling to say thanks.

Just, Just, Just

We use the word "just" in many ways.

We use it to emphasize; as in, "I just want you to clean up your room!" and "It just doesn't work!"

We use the word "just" to try to soften the message; as in, "I'm sorry, we just don't know where your puppy is."

We also use it to mean "only" and that's how telemarketers tend to use it. The trouble is, as in the example above, they really aren't <u>only</u> calling to say thanks or whatever.

Using the word "just" can become a verbal habit. We insert it into so many sentences that we just don't realize we do it. See there? Just like that. Dang! Did it again.

The thing is, your words mean a lot more on the phone than they do in person. In person, words like "just" are hardly noticed. On the phone, the word "just" carries much more meaning.

This fundraiser does not mean "only" and the listener knows that. The disconnect creates a barrier.

"We're calling for <u>three reasons</u>. We want to thank you for your support over the past year. We'd like to tell you what we've done with that support. And we'd like to ask if you would help us again."

This fundraiser needs a three-part message. Saying three things would make for way too long of a sentence. So, the telemarketer says something that <u>sets the stage</u> for saying three things.

The other thing to note here is the fundraiser is ready to say what great things they've accomplished, thanks to support from people like the prospect.

If you're fundraising, avoid scripts that paint a desperate picture or play on people's guilt. Telling people what's going well works far better than telling them how awful things are. You'll get much better results when you point out how every little bit helps.

If you're cold calling for a non-profit or some sort of charity or cause, we suggest you look at the Selling for the Good Witch section. We've got all kinds of neat-o tips for you in that section.

"We see that you haven't activated your new combination calling card and credit card, so I'm going to take care of that for you right now."

If we showed you the entire script for this call, it would be about twelve pages long. It's designed to make it very hard for listeners to get a word in edgewise.

As we pointed out, plenty of us do stop the process. We usually have to be forceful to the point of being rude to do it.

We give you this example to show you the far end of the definitely-don't-do-this spectrum. As you can tell by now, it's far too assumptive. It may even be illegal.

By now, you probably see the trends for a consultative approach. Practice putting this knowledge to work by completing Exercise #1.

Exercise #1 ~ Help!

Script: *"We see that you haven't activated your new combination calling card and credit card, so I'm going to take care of that for you right now."*

a) Prepare to cold-call. Start by writing down your objective:

_____

_____

b) Why not practice the right things, right now? Write down a reward you'll take once you've finished this exercise and have compared your script to ours:

_____

c) Redraft the yucko script shown above:

- Who you are (pretend you're calling from Big Phone, a well-known company).
- Ad.
- Why you're calling (you might want to blend the ad in here).
- Ask permission to proceed.

Keep these points in mind:

- Prospects got this card in the mail because they responded positively to a mail or telemarketing solicitation.

- The card is no good unless it's activated.

- What you'd like to have happen is this: The prospect agrees to activate the card right now on the phone.

d) Compare your version to ours, which is stealthily hidden in the next few pages.

Law: How Would You Want to be Treated?

This seems like a great place to mention legal issues.

There are laws and regulations governing telemarketing, and if you use common sense it's easy to do the right thing. For example, don't call homes before 8 AM or after 9 PM.

Before you get started cold calling, do an internet search for "telemarketing" or "do not call" laws to get details. Learn and follow the regulations that apply to your calling area. (If you find a website you like, you can also refer others to it when needed.)

There are some other things we want to emphasize here:

☑ "Do not call" laws apply to calls made to consumers.

☑ "Do not call" law applies to all calls made to consumers residing in the U.S..

☑ Occasionally, you'll be in a position to educate prospects. Don't get all huffy about their lack of knowledge: help them with information, and see if you need to add them to your own internal "do not call" list.

☑ Laws change often! Check websites regularly.

💣 Though the author believes the "do not call" law is wonderful, she is not an attorney, nor a specialist in telemarketing compliance. Check the above website or with legal counsel!

☞ If you're calling consumers the "do not call" law is a great help. After all, someone who really, really doesn't want to talk with you—so much so that they put their number on the list—is NAP (not a prospect).

☞ If telemarketers hadn't used such a pushy, disrespectful approach for so many years, we wouldn't need these laws, and there'd be no root canal effect!

Meanwhile, Back to Exercise #1

Exercise #1 is a challenge, we know! Here's the original version again:

"We see that you haven't activated your new combination calling card and credit card, so I'm going to take care of that for you right now."

Train Your Brain

Before we look at the script, better check your objective—how you're thinking about what you'd like to have happen.

What you'd like to have happen is that the prospect agrees to activate his or her card right then and there on the phone.

Okay... so much for hopes. What is realistically under your control in this situation? How would you word that in a consultative, permission-requesting way?

☺ You can <u>ask if</u> they are willing, or would like, to activate the card now.

☺ What if they say they don't have the card any more? Then you can <u>ask if</u> they'd like to get the card (again).

Your written objective should include the word "ask."

Or, if you normally use a fancier vocabulary, you should have words that mean "ask," such as "request." And we mean, seriously, if you <u>normally</u> use fancier words.

☎ **Practice writing in your own, normal words!**

Your objective should also include words that help demonstrate you will give prospects the ability to give or withhold permission. You should have used words like:

☺ If
☺ Would like to

Who You Are...

Did you use your first name only, or whole name? Why?

Did you make it clear your last name is not "from Big Phone"?

Your script should include something like, *"My name is Jim and I'm calling from Big Phone."*

☞ Did you write it down!?

How Fabulous!

The next part of the script is the ad. Including an ad is optional. We want you to practice including one so you can decide if ads will work for you.

It might have been very challenging to come up with an ad for a pretend product you know nothing about. On the other hand, you might be a creative genius and have enjoyed that part the most!

At any rate, you might remember that the flow doesn't always go strictly step by step. This script situation is probably one of those times. After all, most people you're pretending to call will have heard all about how cool this combined card is already. That's why we gave you the hint that you might want to blend your ad into the part where you say why you're calling.

You might also want to keep the ad part very simple. So you might end up simply using a word like "convenience." That's what our sample uses and we show that on the next page. However, if you created a separate ad statement, that's great, too!

"I'm Calling Because..."

This is the most important part of the exercise. In fact, if you get this part, but don't do so hot with the rest of the script, you should still pat yourself on the back!

> Adults learn by doing, so practice the whole thing, out loud, for the best results.

You have to be careful to match how you state the reason for your call to the real reason for your call (your objective). If you don't, there will be a hidden agenda eating away at your success!

In addition, you probably need to deal with the fact that (as far as you know) they should have at least received this nifty card.

On the other hand, you have to be careful not to assume they got it, or make it sound like they must be idiots not to have activated it. (People tend not to like being thought of as idiots.)

It might be best to demonstrate you know their life involves lots more than sitting around waiting for the card so they can jump right on the phone and activate it.

Or, finally, you might want to go right to the heart of the matter and ask them if they want to activate the card now.

Here are a few examples of how you might state the reason for your call:

☎ *"We recently sent you our convenient combined calling card/credit card and I'm calling to follow through on a few things. I'd like to make sure you got the card, see if you have any questions about it, and then see if you'd like to activate the card now."*

☎ *"We sent you one of our very convenient combined calling card/credit cards a few days ago and we noticed you haven't activated it yet. I'd like to talk with you about the card and see if you would like to activate it."*

☎ *"We recently sent you one of our great combined calling card/credit cards. If you're like most of our customers, you're busy and may not have had time to activate it. May I activate the card for you now?"*

How did you do, so far?

Please, Sir, May I Say Some More?

Once you've stated the reason for your call, the next thing in your script should be to ask permission to proceed. How you ask permission depends on what you want to do when you get permission to proceed. So, we have to sort of skip down to the rest of the script and then come back to this part…

There are several ways to manage the rest of this call in a consultative manner.

> We'll show you examples of the whole script at the end.

For example, you could check the situation out by asking a bunch of questions. You could ask if they got the card, if they know how to activate it, if they have any questions, etc.

If you go this route, you have to get permission to ask a bunch of questions <u>before</u> you ask them. If you don't, then you're giving listeners a test, assumptive-style.

If you want to ask them questions, your request to proceed should be similar to…

☺ *"I'd like to ask you a few questions, so I know where to start. Is that okay?"*

Another way to handle this call is to start the sale over. In this case, your request for permission might be like this…

☺ *"May I take a minute to go over the benefits of this card, then see if you'd like to activate it?"*

Maybe you think a quick reminder about what happened is a good idea, though. In this case, it might go like this…

☺ *"We see that you haven't activated your new combination calling card and credit card. May I take a minute to remind you about the benefits of the card, then see if you'd like to activate it?"*

Whatever approach you use, you should avoid jumping into what may have happened, as in, *"We sent you a letter about this offer, and you signed up by sending in a postcard."*

The problem with that sort of lecture is it misses the real point of the call. Your ultimate goal is not to find out if they remember the deal they supposedly bought. Saying so would cause a disconnect. What you really want is to see if they want to activate the card now.

One More Train Your Brain

You are almost done with this exercise! What? you exclaim, what else is there to do?

We'll give you two seconds to figure out the last step...

(Take your reward.)

If you completed the exercise, you should now take your reward. And all you had to do was complete the exercise—not get it "right."

Sound weird? Well, did you really have control over matching your script to ours?

Actually, I suppose you could have skipped ahead and checked our version before you got started. Well, so what.

To train your brain, once you complete the exercise, you should take your reward. Do not read on. Stop. Take your reward. Luxuriate in the pleasure of reward and the knowledge that this tiny act will plant seeds of success in your mind.

Of course, if you didn't write stuff down then, you didn't truly complete the exercise so you shouldn't get a reward and we really think you're missing out and if you take a reward that's probably pretty bad karma.

Either way, after showing you a few examples of the whole script (so far), we'll move on to the inside scoop on the next element of successful cold-calling scripts: Qualifying.

How We'd Do It

Okay: From saying who we are, through asking permission to proceed, our script examples looks like this…

☺ *"This is Jim. I'm calling from Big Phone. We recently sent you one of our convenient calling card/credit cards and I'm calling to see if we can follow-through on activating the card.*

Would you like to activate the card?"

☺ *"This is Jim. I'm calling from Big Phone. We see that you haven't activated your new combination calling card/credit card. May I take a minute to remind you about the benefits of the card, then see if you'd like to activate it?"*

☺ *"We recently sent you our convenient combined calling card/credit card and I'm calling to follow through on a few things. I'd like to make sure you got the card, see if you have any questions about it, and then see if you'd like to activate the card now.*

Is that okay?"

"Thrusting my nose firmly between his teeth,
I threw him heavily to the ground on top of me."

Mark Twain, talking about his prospecting methods.

Just How Hot *is* That Prospect?

So you've developed a script that grabs interest and asks permission to proceed. Great! Now the bad news:

Just because you reach a live human who decides to talk with you—no doubt because you are so wonderfully direct and up-front—that doesn't mean you've got a live one.

You might be barking up the wrong tree. Not all contacts will have a good fit with what you're marketing and selling.

Remember, you're not looking for hot <u>sales</u> because that attempts to jump over the whole marketing process. That doesn't work. Try it, and you'll irritate contacts and frustrate yourself.

What you're looking for is good *marketing* fit. This is a fit on a surface level. It's a 'so far, so good' fit.

So how do you know if it's good, so far? Here's how…

"I was gratified to be able to answer promptly.
I said I don't know."

Mark Twain, famous author and psychic.

The Story, So Far…

So far, you've read the inside scoop on these parts of a script to use when talking to contacts/prospects:

- Who you are.
- Ad (optional).
- Why you're calling.
- Request to proceed.

The next part of this script is…

- Information-sharing, including qualifying prospects (which is all about exploring the business marketing fit).

And the last part is…

- Check-in, or requesting to go to the next step.

So What Fits?

First of all, you need to know what characteristics constitute a marketing fit for your business. Second, you have to <u>ask</u> <u>each</u> contact questions about these characteristics so the fit (or lack of one) is known.

Do not guess. Do not presume. Do not spend hours on the internet researching each and every company to try to evaluate the fit in advance.

| Evel Knievel you're not. | And do not attempt to jump over marketing directly into selling. Instead, explore. Evaluate. Go step by step. Pick up the phone and <u>ask</u>. |

What to Ask

We'll use a few examples to illustrate how to identify a good marketing fit, and questions you might use.

- **Savage and Greene** ~ Sales and customer service training and consulting business.

We know we need a minimum of five people who may need training. Companies with fewer than five rarely want to do business.

We know our best bet is to talk with managers responsible for sales or service performance. These are the people who care the most about performance, and usually have budget or the authority to create budget.

We want to know if the manager wants to improve sales or service performance. If they're happy with performance, there's no need for our services! If they are interested in improvement, we need to get a general idea about the issues, so we know if our expertise is a match, or not.

Finally, we want to know if they have used outside resources in the past, or if they'd be open to it. If they're not open to using outside resources, we probably need to talk about train-the-trainer.

 You might wonder why we're not starting by calling human resources or training departments. We often partner with these departments, so we will want to talk with them down the road. However, most of the time they are not our direct client.

You may have a similar situation. Think about all the usual players for your business. Look for the direct client and start your marketing efforts there.

Our telemarketing script for talking with contacts has only 5 qualifying questions:

1. On a scale of 1 to 10, "10" being the best, how would you rate sales (or service) performance?

2. In general terms, what would you want to improve?

3. How many people are in your group?

4. Are you open to using external training services?

We also want to know who else might be involved in making the decision about using services like ours (e.g., Human Resources). We may want to get these people involved in the next step. So, if all the above looks good, we have one more question.

5. If you were to evaluate our services, who else might be involved in that process?

If there are other people involved in the process, we'll do our best to get them involved from the start. You should do this, too.

- **Jasmine Catering ~ Catering business.**

Jasmine Catering has an ad in the yellow pages and they get a lot of calls from people about catering weddings and similar events. However, Jasmine Catering would like to have more corporate events business, so they're telemarketing.

They've discovered that the administrative assistants for senior managers often arrange these events.

They also know catering to match a theme is often important.

And, they know there's a Catch-22: They have to demonstrate reliability or they won't even get a chance to bid.

Jasmine's script for talking with these administrative assistance contacts has only 4 qualifying questions:

1. How many events do you have planned in this year for which you might use catering?

2. Will you be heavily involved in choosing and managing the caterers for these events?

3. Do you have a theme, or type of food identified for these events already?

4. We know that quality and reliability are important. A lot of times, we started earning our clients business with samples. Can we bring some samples to you?

The last question demonstrates knowledge of what's at stake for the prospect and suggests a way around the Catch-22 at the same time.

This last question also uses an effective technique of mentioning "other clients." What your other customers or clients do, say, want, or need will make a better impression than what *you* do, say, want or need.

- **Crystal Communication ~ Telecommunications business.**

Crystal Communication's services apply to both telephone services and computer networks. The sale can be a complicated process. Several meetings, analysis of bills, proposals, and heavy negotiating are often involved.

In these cases, it's tempting to try to shorten the sales process by doing lots of qualifying when marketing. Unfortunately, too many questions can ruin a good marketing call. It doesn't make a good impression and it makes contacts antsy.

You want to use just a handful of questions in telemarketing. If a good business fit for you is rather complex, you're going to have to be extra careful.

Develop questions that give you a fair indication this <u>may</u> be a good business fit. That's all. We gave you one example of this already with Savage and Greene's script. In Crystal Communication's example we'll go a bit further.

Crystal Communication knows their best business fit are companies that will give them <u>all</u> their telecommunications services. They're open to doing pieces of it, but which pieces depends on a lot of variables. So they uncover this issue while telemarketing, but leave handling the variables to the sales process.

Crystal Communication also has a very good sense of which competitors' rates they can beat, and which competitors' services are not rated as highly as their own.

Crystal Communication asks 6 qualifying questions:

1. How many different telecommunications services are you using now?

2. Who do you use for what? (e.g. cellular, networks, land lines.)

3. Of the services you're using, pick the one you're using most dollars-wise and tell me who they are.

4. Most of our clients want to save money and some want to save time. Are any of your current service-providers not making the grade when it comes to service?

5. If we can save you time and money, is there anything that would prevent you from changing any of these services at this time?

Notice the use of "other clients" in question 4!

Crystal Communications also knows their best bet for new clients are those who want more convenience and lower cost for existing services. (Turns out that when companies are looking at new, unfamiliar services, they usually choose bigger-name telecommunications services.)

Crystal Communications wants to know if new services are being planned, so they can explore the chances they'll have a real shot at that business during the sales call. So they also ask:

6.   Are there any telecommunications services you're thinking of adding in the next six months?

Exercise #2 ~ Your Business Fit

We'll give you a chance to script out specific questions that qualify in a bit. In the meantime, jot down thoughts on the characteristics of a good marketing fit for your business.

a. To get the ball rolling, you might jot down the characteristics of:

- Your best client or customer.
- Your average client or customer.
- Clients or customers you don't like to work with, or often lose.

b. Circle the characteristics you want to know about very early on. These are the characteristics of your business marketing fit.

_____

_____

_____

_____

_____

_____

_____

_____

_____

It Fits! What Now?

When the marketing fit is there, you should transition from uncovering information to asking to move on to the next step. The next step will probably be a more in-depth conversation.

You should actually write this transition into your script to make sure it's obvious for both you and the prospect. A transition is something like this:

"Sounds like we may have services of use to you. May I have an appointment to talk more about this?"

It Doesn't Fit. What Now?

There will be lots of times when contacts aren't a good marketing fit. Here are guidelines for what you should do, when:

☎ Right company, wrong person:

Ask who the right person is, and how to reach him or her.

"May I know who I should contact and how to reach that person?"

Train your brain: Consider "wrong" marketing calls a form of networking.

☎ Bad timing:

Ask when you should call again. Then, after they tell you, ask why at that time? This gives you even more information. (We showed you an example of this earlier.)

☎ Doesn't meet minimum fit:

Tell them it doesn't look like your product or services would be a good fit. Yes, tell them! If possible, suggest options.

Then, ask for their suggestions for other organizations you might try. If they give you suggestions, ask if you can use their name when you call.

"Doesn't look like we'd be the right vendor for you. I'd like to suggest you contact ABC Cleaning Services. Would you like their number?

Do you have any suggestions of other companies I might call on?

May I tell them you suggested I call?"

☎ They adore their current whatever:

You have a choice to make here: (A) You might ask if they're interested in meeting to exchange information on a possible just-in-case basis, or for networking.

"Thanks for telling me you're not open to a new provider. Would you be willing to talk more for possible future reference?"

"Thanks for telling me. I wonder, would you be interested in getting to know each other's businesses a bit more? We might make good referral sources for each other."

Or, (B) you might say thanks and move on.

💣 Do not slam their current whatever in any way. This never, ever looks good on you.

Words of Wisdom About Qualifying

Once again, we will take a moment to impart some great truths about marketing and selling. This part is important. You might want to put it under your pillow for subliminal learning.

☎ Someone who won't talk with you *at all* is not a good challenge—they're not a prospect!

N.A.P.
Not
A
Prospect

Let go. Move on. Call back later.

☎ Luck *does* play a part in telemarketing.

You can up your chances by telemarketing consistently. However, you will always miss some and that's no reflection on you. If you missed an opportunity due to timing, shrug it off.

☎ Stay away from too much information-gathering in telemarketing.

You should have only a handful of qualifying questions. If things are looking good, then transition to whatever you need to prepare for a great sales call. Here's an example from Crystal Communication:

"Based on what you've told me, we can save you some money. I'd like to set up an appointment so we can discuss this in greater detail. May I meet with you?

When is a good time to meet?

Great. I'll need the last three months of bills from the telecommunications services you're using now so we can prepare a quote. See you at 3 PM on the 10th, then."

☎ The one thing you can always count on is change.

People change jobs. Organizations change focus. Current vendors mess up. Things happen!

This means the N.A.P. today may be a hot prospect tomorrow. Put non-prospects on the back burner and give them a call from time to time.

On to Scripting

Now it's time to put these pieces of information to work for *your* cold calling scripts.

The way you put this to work is to write things out, so the next section—yes, you guessed it—covers this.

"No passion in the world is equal
to the passion to alter someone else's draft."

H. G. Wells, a guy who is often confused with Orson Welles,
who is often confused with William Randolph Hearst.

Scripting à la You

Now that we've covered key concepts, we're about to give you lots of practice in applying them to <u>your</u> business.

In this section we cover how you can draft scripts for three different purposes:

- Finding information (gatekeeper script).
- Marketing (contact script).
- Voicemail.

One thing you'll probably notice is we want you to write these scripts down. You might wonder how writing things down jibes with our earlier advice about making successful consultative calls: We said you should avoid sounding canned—that you should be yourself.

That's still true. We do want you to be yourself. We also want you to be able to write "yourself" down. Read on to find out why.

"He can compress the most words
into the smallest idea of any man I ever met."

Abraham Lincoln, possibly talking about an annoying telemarketer,
except for the fact that telephones weren't invented yet.

The Power of the Pen

Adults learn by doing, in action. The process of writing, all by itself, is an action that helps you apply the information and concepts in this book.

Since reading this book constitutes self-study, the only other ways to learn by doing would be to role-play by yourself or actually telemarket.

Using either of these methods, you'd have to somehow pay close attention to what you say and how you say it; as you make bunches and bunches of calls; then analyze what worked and what didn't; and make changes accordingly. Ack!

☎ Writing things down gives you a shortcut to success.

There's another reason to write things down. Using well-written scripts frees you to easily handle the nuances of communication. Your natural ability to hear and use subtle differences in tone and slight changes in phrasing kicks in.

The Problem with the Pen

There is a catch. Most of write more formally than we speak. For example, if I were saying that out loud, I'd probably say, "Most of us write more formally than we *talk*."

It will take a bit of practice to get the hang of writing scripts that match the real you.

☎ To make sure your scripts sound like the real you, test-drive them on a friend or co-worker. Does it sound like the relaxed, natural you?

"Didn't you see the sign!? "

The gatekeeper of Oz, who responded to the bell, but insists Dorothy, et al, must now knock.

Gatekeepers, Your New Best Friend

A "gatekeeper" is any person who picks up the phone before you can be connected to a contact.

A gatekeeper might be a receptionist, an operator, or any ole person who happens to pick up the phone.

Unfortunately, lots of telemarketers think gatekeepers are out to keep them from the goodies. These telemarketers try to sneak by gatekeepers, or manipulate them, or even scare them. This doesn't work very well. Besides, that's not your style, right?

"The reverse side also has a reverse side."

Japanese proverb, possibly coined by very good procrastinators.

Why We Love Gatekeepers

Gatekeepers are your strongest telemarketing ally. Gatekeepers can and will:

- ☑ Tell you who you should try to reach and how to reach them.
- ☑ Help you reach people who aren't calling you back.
- ☑ Help you avoid wasting your time.

This is especially true for bona fide receptionists, operators, and administrative assistants. These guys (okay, they're mostly women) know who does what and how to get in touch with them. They have to! It's their job to leverage these resources.

Getting these people to help you is easy. You ask. You see, the other cool thing about gatekeepers is they are natural helpers. That's a big part of their job, too.

Managing the Ever-Changing List

One reason you'll work with gatekeepers a lot has to do with lists. You might recall we blew apart the myth of "great" telemarketing lists in the first section. They simply don't exist. People move around too much and organizations change the way they do business too often for fixed data to be completely accurate.

A good list gives you an excellent start, which saves you lots of time and effort. Still, you can expect to spend time simply making changes to existing lists.

You may also need to build your own lists from scratch. You might start by noting a company name in a newspaper. From there, you'll probably have to make several calls to find who your best contact is and how to reach that person.

Who helps you do all this? Gatekeepers!

What do You Really, Really Want?

Before you call gatekeepers and ask for help, you should have a good idea of what sort of help you want. Look over the list below and make a mental check for each need you might have.

- ☐ Do you want help in identifying who you should contact?
- ☐ Do you want suggestions for an alternate contact?
- ☐ Maybe you're striking out with the contact: Do you want suggestions for better ways or times to reach him or her?
- ☐ Do you want to gather some information about the company?
- ☐ Do you want to confirm information?

Who are You Looking for?

You should also be ready to describe your best contact concisely. Think about:

- ☐ Who usually buys from you?
- ☐ What are their usual titles?
- ☐ What kind of work do these folks usually do? Or what department might they be in?

No Usually for Ya?

You may find there is no usual contact for your business at all. Maybe job titles vary a lot. Maybe the organizations make purchases out of different departments. If this is the case, you want to be ready to work with each organization individually.

Stay clear of titles and departments. Instead, describe your best contact in general terms and let the gatekeeper take it from there.

Example:

"Hi, my name is Peter Jones and I could use your help in figuring out who I should talk to. Can I tell you a little bit about why I'm calling and get your suggestion on who I should talk to?"

(Gatekeeper says, "Sure.")

"I work for Crystal Communications. I'd like to talk with the person who manages your phone and networks to see if we might have services of use to you. Who would that be?"

(Gatekeeper says, "That would be Jim Davis, our systems manager.")

Focus on One Thing at a Time

You'll have more telemarketing success when you focus on one objective at a time.

Be a Zen Master: Use the flow of the moment.

Focusing on one objective at a time gets you into the flow of the process. You'll be more efficient and effective. That goes for building or updating lists, too.

If you're building a list, then your objective is to build your list. Once you have a contact name and phone number, don't ask to be connected. Just say "thanks" and hang up.

Then, call the contacts in a separate calling session because you have a separate objective.

Of course, this is not a hard and fast rule—there aren't any of those. If you're put through to the contact before you can say thanks and hang up, by all means, go for it!

All I Want is to Get Through

Aside from building lists, the other time you'll talk with gatekeepers is when calls go through a central number.

Maybe the operator won't give you the direct number. Maybe the person you want to talk to has their own special phone-answerer. Maybe everyone in the company answers the phone.

In this situation, it's easy to get frustrated. Don't they remember me? you might think.

Other times, it may seem like everyone is trying to protect everyone else from you—the terrible, sleazy, waste-their-time telemarketer.

But, wait! You're not that kind of telemarketer! So don't act like one.

☎ Be direct and up-front about the reason for your call.
☎ Give them a context for the call, if necessary.
☎ Ask to be put through.

Here's an example of how this works, with a complex, incredibly detailed analysis matrix:

Who you are...	*"My name is Harold.*
Context, and why you're calling...	*I understand Rocky Cooper is your paper buyer. I'd like to talk with him about what our company offers in this area, and see if we may have a good business fit.*
Ask to be put through...	*May I speak with Rocky?"*

Your Turn

You can go right to work on your own gatekeeper script by skipping to Exercise #3. Or, check out the following examples for some inspiration.

Gatekeeper Examples

☎ *"My name is Shawn. I have a business that specializes in sales training. I'd like to ask your help to find out who I should contact about a possible fit for our services. May I ask you a few questions?*

- *Does (company) have a sales force?*
- *Who manages that sales force?*
- *What is the best way to reach this person?*

Don't know a thing about this company?

Thank you very much!"

☎ *"Hi, this is Sarah. I'm calling from YYZ Enterprises. We do project management. I'd like to confirm some general information I have about this company. It will take just a second; may I ask you a couple questions?*

- *Does this company have more than 1,000 employees?*
- *May I have the name of your Human Resources manager? I'd like to talk with him or her about our services.*

A quick qualifier.

Thanks. Have a great day!"

☎ *"This is Richard Lind. I'm calling from Rich Financial Services. I've been trying to reach Jason Andrews to talk with him about our financial planning services.*

So far, I haven't been able to reach him. Can I impose on you for a suggestion on how to reach him at his desk?

Before you put a contact on a back burner, see if you can get some help.

Thanks for your help."

Tips for Inhuman Operators

Lots of organizations have computer systems that answer the phone for them. These systems are apparently designed by evil programmers who live to frustrate both customers and telemarketers. Never fear, there's hope. Here's what to do:

☎ Try pressing "0" or "00." This often gets you to a human with a directory. (You can also try this when you get voicemail.)

☎ You might ask the operator-type person if your contact can be paged. Warning! Some contacts won't mind pages at all, and others will go ballistic.

☎ Try dialing any ole extension or choosing any ole person from the directory. Then ask for their help. Be extra-grateful: This is not their job!

☎ If they have a customer service or sales line, try calling that and ask for help.

If all the above fails, give up for now. Someone you can't even reach is not a good challenge, they're definitely not a good prospect. Move on to make room for your next successful contact!

☞ Recently, the phone companies have come up with a new service that announces you, and gives the person on the other end of the line the option to pick-up or not. You can use part of your voicemail script, to announce yourself. See that section ☺

Exercise #3 ~ Gatekeepers

a) Draft your own gatekeeper script. Here's the format you should follow:

Who you are.
Why you're calling.
Ask for help and/or request to proceed.
Description of likely contacts, just in case.
Thank you.

b) Say it out loud. How does it sound to you?

c) Now test-drive on a friend, co-worker, or real gatekeeper.

d) Adjust your draft, if necessary and test-drive it again.

Well, Hi There!

Before we cut you loose on creating terrific scripts for talking with actual live contacts, we better quickly remind you what "success" is.

Of 100 dials…

You'll reach 33 live humans…

11 of those people will talk with you <u>and</u> have a good business fit…

And that's as far as this picture should go, to keep your focus in the right place.

"You might as well fall flat on your face as lean over too far backward."

James Thurber, humor writer and former contortionist.

Contacts: On to the Big Shew

There are a couple basic formats that will probably work for your scripts for contacts.

Format A:

- ☑ Who you are.
- ☑ Ad (optional).
- ☑ Why you're calling.
- ☑ Request to proceed.
- ☑ Information sharing—including qualifying contact.
- ☑ Check in, or request to go to next step.

Format B:

- ☑ Who you are.
- ☑ Ad (optional).
- ☑ Why you're calling.
- ☑ What you need to know.
- ☑ Next-steps.

The big difference between these two formats is that the second one doesn't give the contact much information about what you're selling.

Of course, there are pros and cons to each format.

Check out the contrasting examples and pointers on the next couple pages. This will help you decide which you want to use.

Format A

"My name is Laurel and I'm calling from Quantum Audio Video Services. We make meetings more meaningful! I'd like to exchange a little information, then see if it makes sense for us to talk at greater length.

Is that okay with you?

Don't ask, "Is this a good time?"

We provide on-call audio and visual services. We bring in whatever equipment you might need to have terrific presentations, run them to make sure it all goes smoothly, and clean it all up afterward.

Now I'd like to ask you a few questions. Is that okay?

- *How many important meetings do you usually hold each year?*
- *Do you use AV equipment now?*

- *If your organization were to add AV to your meetings…*
- *If your organization were change how you handle AV…would you be involved in looking into that?*

Based on what you've told me, I think we might have some services of use to you. Are you open to setting up a meeting?

Would you prefer a phone, or in-person meeting?

Great. I'll send you one of our brochures, and I'll call you on…"

Pointers About Format A

☎ Laurel doesn't use her last name because her first name is unusual. Using just her first name helps people hear and 'get' it.

☎ Laurel has an ad to describe what her business does. Using an ad is optional. You should create some ads and experiment with using them.

☎ The line that asks permission to proceed is written separately. That's to make sure Laurel asks—and gets a yes—before moving on. Stay far, far away from rhetorical questions (questions you ask, but don't wait for an answer).

☎ You might notice there is no "trial close." Trial closes don't work very well in telemarketing any more because they are too close to assuming a sale. Trial closes are also a very transparent technique that screams, "canned!"

☎ Laurel has written down alternative ways to ask the last qualifying question so she can be flexible without having to wing it.

☎ Very importantly, she doesn't use an assumptive close to try and go to the next step. She asks the prospect (yes, it's a real prospect now) if he wants to meet.

Format B

"My name is Laurel and I'm calling from Quantum Audio Video Services. We make meetings more meaningful! I'd like to ask you a few quick questions to see if our services might have a good fit for your business.

> The ad line would have to say more if the company name didn't have "audio video services" in it.

May I ask you a few questions?

- *How many important meetings do you usually hold each year?*
- *Do you use AV equipment now?*

- *If your organization were to add AV to your meetings…*
- *If your organization were change how you handle AV…would you be involved in looking into that?*

Thanks for that information. I'd like the opportunity to tell you about our services and to explore a business fit in more detail. Are you open to meeting?

Would you prefer a phone, or in-person meeting?

Great, I'll see you on…"

Pointers About Format B

☎ This version is more on the assumptive side because it doesn't give the listener much information. In fact, Laurel didn't give the listener any real information at all!

☎ When you use this type of call, you tend to get a "yes" from prospects who are thinking about services like yours. This means you lucked out on timing and therefore these prospects may be hotter.

☎ This approach also gets more "no's" because it is more assumptive.

Which version works better? Depends, of course. We like the first version better, ourselves. The first version gives contacts more information and therefore more reasons to be interested. Test drive the version that seems most comfortable to you, first.

To Ad, or Not to Ad?

No, this isn't a mathematical story problem, we swear! Using an ad is a great way to catch people's attention. However, it's also fairly common for an ad to sound forced or inappropriate.

We recommend that you create a few ads, then test-drive them on colleagues, friends, and real prospects. If the ads sound good, go for it! If using an ad doesn't fit—let it go.

For tips on creating ads, see the advice on our website on "30 second elevator" speeches.

Your Turn

You'll soon see an exercise cleverly designed for drafting your very own script for contacts. Before you get started, we have some words of advice:

☎ You may find you need lots of drafts for this script. Writing the way you talk takes practice.

☎ Keep your sentences short. This helps you take breaths in-between and sound natural and relaxed.

☎ Write down everything! That includes the lines where you ask permission to proceed, or check-in with the prospect. This helps ensure a consultative call.

☎ Don't get all fancy with a bunch of "If yes" and "If no" and "If sort of interested" with arrows and graphs and stuff to organize your script. Keep it simple!

☎ For now, script for "yes" only. Figure out how to deal with objections later.

☎ However, do script a request to call back if you hear a "no." Put this at the very bottom of your script.

If you don't already have a quick ad statement, create at least one. Focus on the <u>end-result</u> of what your products or services do for customers.

☎ Test-drive your scripts on someone who knows you. Does it sound really truly like the regular you?

☎ Some people do better when their scripts show all the words. Some people do better with bullet-points.

As long as the bullets prompt you to say the <u>whole</u> thing, time after time, bullets are fine. If not, then you'll have to take the time to write the whole thing out for the most success.

☎ You might draft out your whole script, then as soon as you read it outloud it suddenly sounds like… you know. That's just part of the process. Draft again!

☎ It's possible that you could draft out your whole script, read it outloud, then as soon as you actually pick up the phone you know it won't work. That's just part of the process. Draft again!

Exercise #4 ~ Contact

a) Set a reward you'll take when you've completed this exercise.

b) Draft your script.

    We're showing you format A for this exercise. It's the easiest to start with and may be the most successful for you, anyway.

    Who you are.
    Ad (not optional, for exercise).
    Why you're calling.
    Request to proceed.
    Information sharing, including qualifying prospects.
    Transition. Ask for a meeting, or for a next-step.

    (Who else might you call?)

c) After you complete your draft, be sure to say it out loud—to someone else, if possible. Does it sound like the real you?

    You might need to say it out loud a few times to both get the hang of it and make sure it sounds like the normal you.

d) If needed, draft again and test-drive again.

    We've got script examples for you on the next couple pages. Try to complete the exercise before looking at them, unless you are really, really stuck.

e) Take your reward!

Who	*My name is Carlos. I'm calling from Systems Simpler.*
Ad	*We make sure our clients and their computers live happily ever after.*
Why	*I'm calling to see if our maintenance services might work well for your organization.*
Permission	*Can I tell you a bit about Systems Simpler, then ask you a few questions?*
Exchange information (you go first)	*We've been in business for five years. We work with companies that don't have their own internal tech support departments and companies whose tech departments are over-loaded. We don't require a long term service agreement. Our clients say they like how fast we get on-site and get them back up and running.*
Transition	*That's a bit about us. Now I have a few questions for you.*
What do you need to know?	*Tell me about the types of computers you have in your company. For example, does everyone have a PC, or MAC? Do you have a network?*

- *Do you have an internal tech support department?*
- *Do you have a service agreement with an outside vendor?*

> *How long does it usually take them to get to you and fix the problem?*

Transition. Ask for meeting or next step.	*Sounds like we might come in handy sometime. I'd like to talk more about your support. Can we meet?*
	No fit: Sounds like you're getting what you need from (internal or external). May I check back with you? When should I call? Any particular reason why in (time given)?

Who	*My name is Jill. I'm calling from ABC Printers.*
Ad	*We love to put you on paper.*
Why	*I'd like to explore the possibility we could earn your printing business.*
Permission	*May I go on?*
Exchange information (you go first)	*We're a full service print shop, catering to businesses such as yours. We have the tools and know-how you need to create printed materials. About half of our clients think we're fabulous because we handle it all for them and free them up to focus on their business. And about half think we're fabulous because we partner so well with them.*
Transition	*That's us! Now, a few questions for you.*
What do you need to know?	*When it comes to printing, what do you want most: a printer who frees you up, or a partner?* *Tell me a little bit about the reasons behind that preference.* *Please give me an overview of your most common printing needs and how you fill them now. (Which printer do you use most often?)*
Transition. Ask for meeting or next step.	*I think we might have a good business fit and I'd like to explore that further. Can we meet so I can show you samples and we can talk more?* *If you were to use a new printer, who else might be involved in that decision? Can (whoever) join us in our meeting?* No fit: *Doesn't sound like we've got a fit right now. Do you have suggestions of associates I might contact? Is it okay with you if I check back with you later?*

Who	*My name is Sam and I'm calling from Merit Temp Agency.*
Ad	*We help you with the human side of business.*
Why	*I'm calling to find out if our services would be of use to you.*
Permission	*May I give you a quick "ad" for Merit, then ask you a couple questions?*
Exchange information (you go first)	*We know you get lots of calls from temp agencies, so here's the short and sweet of it: We believe it's the people we send to work for you that counts most. Our temps are reliable, good workers who can actually complete the tasks you need done.*
Transition	*Here's what I'd like to ask you:*
What do you need to know?	*Do you use temporary workers?*
	(No.) *Do you see any future use of temporary workers?*
	What's the best way for us to demonstrate we deserve your business?
Transition. Ask for meeting or next step.	(3 scripted responses, based on past experience of what prospects say to last question.)

- *I'd be happy to give you client references. Here are three... When should I follow up with you?*

- *So I need to check back with you. When should I do that? Any special reason why (when)?*

- *Is there an order for a temp I can take now?*

If no fit: *Thanks for the information. Doesn't look like we can be of help to you. Can I impose on you for suggestions for others to call?*

Who

Ad

Why

Permission

Exchange information (you go first)

Transition

What do you need to know?

Transition. Ask for meeting or next step.

The Best Part

You might think you just completed the best part (or the most important part) of this book. Not so. Well, not necessarily.

It's true that learning how to script for talking with real, live contacts is very important. On the other hand, doing that well only gets you so far. You really do have to know how to work with gatekeepers and how to prevent frustration to have outstanding success. Hopefully, you read through those sections and completed those exercises, in which case, you are indeed ready to go!

But, Wait…

Are you so psyched up now that you want to grab that phone and start calling? Great! And before you do, remember what we said about expectations for reaching people live on the phone…

"No."

President Jimmy Carter's daughter Amy's response to a reporter's
question about any message she'd like to share with the nation's children.

You're Gonna Love Voicemail!

We believe voicemail is the greatest thing since sourdough bread was invented. And now that you've worked your way through scripting for gatekeepers and contacts, you're going to find that scripting for voicemail is easy.

Putting aside the fact that sourdough bread has little to do with telemarketing, here's how to use this fabulous tool.

"I really didn't say everything I said."

Yogi Berra. Nuf said.

Keep Your Focus

Remember that telemarketing is *marketing*. The point of marketing is to get your prospects' attention. You don't have to reach them live to do this.

Out of 100 dials, you should expect to get as many as 67 voicemail opportunities. You can have even more opportunities if you market during off hours—and you might want to do that on purpose!

Use the Power of Voice

Your tone of voice and the words you use have a huge impact when you're on the phone. All you need to take full advantage of voicemail is to harness that power by preparing a good script and using it.

A great voicemail script includes these elements:

 Who you are.
Ad.
Why you're calling.
Call to action.
What you'll do next.
Who you are, again, and how to reach you.

Hey, This Looks Familiar!

The majority of your voicemail script—the most important parts—will probably be very close to the first part of your script for contacts. For example, let's hear from Laurel again.

"My name is Laurel and I'm calling from Quantum Audio Video Services. We make meetings more meaningful! I'd like to explore the possibility we might have a good business fit."

So far, this voicemail message says who she is, where she's calling from, gives that dandy ad line, and says what she wants. This is very similar to the first part of her script for contacts.

What's Different

In her contact script (format A), Laurel <u>also</u> says she wants to talk at greater length, if it makes sense to do that.

On voicemail, since she's not actually talking live with the contact, that sounds funny. Or does it? Here's what it would read like:

"My name is Laurel and I'm calling from Quantum Audio Video Services. We make meetings more meaningful. I'd like to exchange a little information, then see if it makes sense for us to talk at greater length."

Would this work for voicemail? Before you decide, read on…

Aaaand…Action!

There's a thing in marketing called a "call to action." The idea is whenever you use a passive marketing tool—whenever you won't be personally present to deal with each prospect's reaction—you try to drive their reaction.

That's why direct mail has things like, "Act now!" on the envelope. The thinking is that when we see commands, we'll jump right on it.

Though the "call to action" theory was created many, many years ago, at a time when we were actually thrilled to get mail and believed everything in print, it still seems to work.

You want to do what you can to get listeners to respond to your voicemail. So, give a "call to action" and use the same consultative, non-assumptive style you do with the rest of your calls.

What should you suggest the listener do? You might suggest they:

☎ Check out your website.
☎ Look for something you're sending them in the mail.
☎ Call you back!

Do Be a Do Bee

In addition to telling them what you want them to do, you should tell them what you'll do next. This helps increase their memory of your call.

There are only two things you should do: You'll either:

- Call them again soon,
- or call them again later.

Either way, you should tell them so in your message.

"I'll try you again in about a week. In the meantime, you might want to check out our website at www.greatcompany.com."

> Avoid exact timeframes for your call back. It's not necessary, and can put you in a corner.

And here's what you might say when you'll be calling them much later:

Well, this is my third try for reaching you. My guess is employee benefits aren't a hot topic right now, so I'll follow up less often. If you'd like to reach me, Jon Paul, at Andrews Associates, feel free to call me at 510.237.8323."

Hot Tips for Voicemail

☎ Most voicemail systems give you up to two minutes of message. Too long! Your voicemail should be about 30 seconds long.

Test-drive with a timer to see how long it is.

☎ Repeat your name at the end of the message. Give them your phone number.

When you say these, speak s l o w l y .

☎ Don't give an exact timeframe for your call-back. Exact timeframes are unnecessary and can be a trap for you.

"I'll call again in a week or so. In the meantime, feel free to contact me, Gail Smith, at…"

(Yes, we put this tip in twice.)

☎ Don't expect them to call you back.

Keep your focus on the right place. You are marketing. Your objective in leaving the voicemail is not to get them to call you back, it's to get their attention. That's all. That's it.

That's plenty, because they are more likely to remember you when you call again.

☎ Be prepared for them to call you back! A really great voicemail that comes at the right time, to the right person, will get you a call back.

This is one more reason for matching up your script, list and objective. If you tailored your script to each and every prospect, then you'd have to recall the details when they called back!

It's okay if you don't remember every single prospect you called. You're human and if they are unhappy with that—N.A.P.

"Remind me: Did I call with my prospecting hat on?"

☎ If you call early or late, don't bother with a reason.

You don't need to explain why you're calling at an unusual time. Besides, if you don't explain, then when prospects call you back, they will often ask you about it and that makes for a nice icebreaker.

Remember to check rules about telemarketing hours, especially if you're calling consumers. (After 8 AM and before 9 PM.)

☎ Use your outgoing voicemail as an ad space, too.

Think about it: Do you really need to explain you're away from your desk, on the other line, using the internet, unable to come to the phone, that they should leave a message at the tone…blah blah blah? No! So use that space for an ad.

The exceptions to this great advice are:

- When you're not going to check voicemail very often, or at all; as in on vacation.

- When callers often need help NOW. If this is the case, give them another person and/or number to call.

☎ If there is a way to skip the outgoing message and to right to recording, tell us at the start of the message—not at the end.

☎ Use a second mailbox for tips or special announcements.

☎ Change your outgoing message every few months or so—or even more often. This practice helps keep the message fresh and makes you practice your "elevator" speech.

Very Hot Tips for Very Small Business

☎ If you have a very small business and want to sound very successful, have a person of the opposite gender record your outgoing message.

Make sure your message says "we" or the business name, instead of "I."

The same goes for consultants. Sure, you're on your own, but don't you want to sound oh so successful and busy that you can't possibly pick up the phone? So have your "assistant" record the outgoing message.

☎ Get voicemail!

Voicemail is cheap; has a very clear sound; picks up calls when you can't; gives more time for outgoing and incoming messages—to name just a few great features.

Message machines almost always sound rinky dink. Not to mention, few successful businesses use machines any more. Which image do you want?

☎ Avoid blending your personal message-taking with business. So, none of this kind of stuff, "You can also leave a message for Jenny and Biff, our dog, too."

If you need to have a personal line, get a mailbox and say something like, "Press 2# for the Smith household."

Voicemail Examples

☎ *"My name is Dennis O'Leary and I'm calling from Winners Trophy Company. Want to celebrate something? We've got just the thing!*

I'm going to put a brochure in the mail to you, and try you again next week. Please keep your eyes open for it. This is Dennis O'Leary, with Winners Trophy Company. You can reach me at 454.222.1234."

☎ *"This is Linda. I'm calling from Jasmine Catering. We do great food, on time, with a smile! I'm hoping to talk with you about how we might get a chance to cater one of your events.*

I'll try you again in a few days. In the meantime, you can call Jim at Monster Construction and ask about our services. His number is 415.457.9090. My name again is Linda. My number at Jasmine Catering is 510.788.2345."

Outgoing Voicemail Examples

☎ *"This is Theresa, with ABC Information Services. Our knowledge management software puts know-how at your fingertips. You can skip the rest of this message, which is about my travel schedule, by pressing the # button now…"*

☎ *"Hi! You've reached Systems Simpler and Lesley Coral's voicemail. I can help you and your computer live happily ever after. Leave your message, or—if you're about to throw that PC out the window—press OO and tell our operator you need help right away."*

Your turn!

Exercise #5 ~ Voicemail

a)   Set a reward.

b)   Create your voicemail script. Feel free to draw from the script you just drafted for contacts. Follow this format:

Who you are.
Ad.
Why you're calling.
Call to action.
What you'll do next.
Who you are, again, and how to reach you.

b) Script a voicemail for calling much later, too. The idea is you're putting this prospect on a back burner. If you tell them this in your message, they'll be more likely to remember you when you do call back…later.

The format is:

Who you are.
Ad.
Why you're calling.
Call to action.
What you'll do next.
Who you are, again, and how to reach you.

c) To test-drive these voicemail drafts, call yourself and leave a message.

d) Finally, script an outgoing voicemail message and record it on your phone.

f)   Have someone call you to tell you how it sounds.

g)   Take your reward!

Managing to Succeed

So far, you've learned a lot about making great consultative cold calls.
You've also learned quite a bit about preventing frustration. Now it's time to
learn how to <u>keep</u> your telemarketing success rolling!

"I just hitch up my girdle and let it rip."

Babe Zaharias' answer to a question about how she managed
to play golf so well, considering the awful handicap of being a woman.

How Many Dials?

You might recall that it's important to focus on where you are in the marketing and sales process. You're at the very top of the funnel. Your goal? To make a certain number of calls. So, how many calls should you make?

There are a couple ways to set effective dials goals: Using time or using math.

Time

Let's say you set aside 4 hours per week for telemarketing.

☎ You should not make calls for more than one hour at a time, at the *very* most.

☎ You can make about 30 dials in one hour, on average.

Let's say you decide to telemarket one hour per day, four days a week. So your dials goal for each of these calling sessions is only 30. (Use 25 to get started.)

You could also focus an entire half-day (4 hours) on telemarketing. So your dials goal for this calling session is 120. (Use 100 to get started.) Remember to stop every 45 minutes to an hour for a short break.

☎ Track each session separately, so you can find out if certain days of the week, or time of day, works better for you.

☞ Need a tracking sheet? There's a sample in the back of the book. You can also email us to get a full-size version.

Math

You can also use the end result (new business) to drive your dials goal. This is where the expression, "Sales is a numbers game," comes from. It doesn't mean we regard prospects as faceless numbers, or that all you have to do is call and call and you'll succeed. It means there are mathematical equations we can use to define our marketing efforts and help measure success.

The illustration on the facing page shows you three things:

☎ How to calculate effective dials goals:

- Use left side of the funnel to calculate your dials goal.
- Start at the bottom of the funnel.
- Multiply each step by 3.

☎ What you can expect to have happen, on average.

The figures on the right show you what will probably happen, over time, on average. Use these figures to help set your expectations.

☎ And what is the measure of success.

Use the figures on the right to pinpoint problems and successes.

But watch out! Don't let yourself slip into comparing your results for every calling session. That not only misses the whole point of "average," it's probably your subconscious' sneaky way of giving you supposedly good reasons not to pick up the phone and do what you should be doing.

Danger! Will Robinson, Danger!

"Huh!?" You may notice that we've mentioned "3 to 5" closed sales several times, in the last 120 pages or so. But, the figure to the right is only "3." What's up?

Math, that's what. If you start at the top of the funnel, and divide; you get a different number than if you start at the bottom, and multiply.

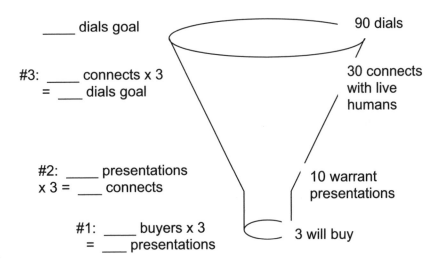

| Calculate Dials Goals | Expectations/Success |

_____ dials goal — 90 dials

#3: _____ connects x 3 = ___ dials goal — 30 connects with live humans

#2: _____ presentations x 3 = ___ connects — 10 warrant presentations

#1: _____ buyers x 3 = ___ presentations — 3 will buy

Almost Algebra

Here's another way to figure out how many dials to make:

Step 1:   Choose a number for new business. Call this NB.

Step 2:   Multiply NB by 3. Call this P (presentations).

Step 3:   Multiply P by 3. Call this C (connects).

Step 4:   Multiply C by 3. This is your dials goal.

Example: NB = 3.
            3 x 3 = 9.
            9 x 3 = 27.
            27 x 3 = 81.   81 is the dials goal.

Jeez, Look at all Those Dials...

If you're like most people, you're looking at this equation and thinking, "Three sales out of 90 calls?" and a root canal is looking pretty good, once again.

Keep in mind the calculation is not only based on averages, it's based on making absolutely freezing cold calls. Chances are good that you will make warmer calls and your results will be better.

Warm Things Up

Here's what you can do to make your calls warmer:

☎ Have a strong sense of your best customer and call on prospects that match that picture.

For example, if your best customer has at least 100 employees, don't call on sole proprietors.

☎ Know who your best contacts usually are. Go for a buyer: One of the person who has budget and/or authority to make the purchase.

For example, if you're selling project management software, call on the mucky mucks whose departments manage projects.

☎ When you reach the wrong person, ask for their help in finding the right person.

For example, if one of our contacts says they never ever use outside training resources, we ask the contact to suggest other departments or companies we should try.

Calculate Your Own Success

It bears repeating that your own telemarketing results may be different from the figures shown above.

Use tracking sheets (sample at back of book), accumulate a bunch, and use the information to figure out your averages.

It also bears repeating that if your results are not at least as good as the figures shown above, something needs fixing. See the troubleshooting section.

I've Got to Sell Something!

Do you remember that a ways back…about 70 pages or so…we mentioned that your cold calling goal should not be a sales number? We said that you should focus on where you are in the process—marketing—to prevent frustration.

Well, let's face it, unless your job is to generate leads, you're not in the business of merely marketing. Sales have got to happen. This will be on your mind, at some level, even while you focus on what you need to accomplish to get there.

So, the challenge is to satisfy your desire to make sales in a way that still lets you focus on marketing. Luckily, the solution is simple:

✎ Write. Mark off calls and make notes as you telemarket.

Your Secret Weapon

Again with the writing thing! you exclaim. Yes, again with the writing thing. (And, no, we don't own stock in an ink or pencil company.)

When you mark off calls as you make them, the action and the mark itself sends a message of progress to your brain. *Look!* your eyes say, *we have done something. We have made calls. We are ever closer to achieving our dials goal, which will get us to our sales goal. We are inspired to keep going.*

Marking off calls and taking notes during each call engages both hemispheres of your brain. You'll be quicker, more creative, and possibly more energized.

Use your whole brain by writing.

Marking off calls also helps you switch gears. The small hand movement is enough to help you let go of the last call and focus on the next.

Finally, marking off calls creates the data you need to complete your unique success calculation. Any other method is merely a PFA (pulled from air).

It's not hard to put all of the above to work when you use a tracking sheet. You don't need a formal form, either. You can use scratch paper and show:

- Date (day of week and time are useful, as well).
- Dials goal.
- Reward.
- Place to mark off:
  Dials
  Voicemail
  Connects
  Next Step or Objective reached
  NAP (includes wrong numbers)

Are We There Yet?

Okay, so you're setting marketing goals and marking calls off as you go. Still, there's something missing, isn't there? There are days when you're not quite satisfied. The joys of voicemail ring hollow. You find yourself thinking about dental work...

What you need is some instant gratification. You need a reward.

Before you start each calling session, set a reward for yourself. Write it on your tracking sheet somewhere.

Good rewards take about ten minutes. Here are some rewards our clients have put to good use:

- Call a friend.
- Watch the soaps for ten minutes.
- Walk around the block.
- Ice cream!
- Play solitaire for ten minutes.
- Sit in car, play music really loud and sing.

In case you're wondering, "getting appointments" or "follow-through on prospects" are not appropriate rewards.

More Train Your Brain

Some people keep going past their dials goal when they are having a great session. Some people grit their teeth and keep calling past their dials goal when they are having a terrible session. Please don't do *either* of those things.

Meeting dials goals focuses you on the right behavior: making dials. Taking rewards gives you needed instant gratification. If you bypass either of these, you sabotage the process of building new successful habits and attitude.

Attitudes change when behavior changes—not the other way around.

☎ **After you make your last call, stop:** Take your reward, and take a break!

Should You *Ever* Quit?

You will have days when you don't reach a single pleasant human being who is also a good prospect. These days are extremely rare, so keep going until you meet your dials goal.

However, there are times when you should quit on a calling session. For example, if you are so stressed or distracted that you cannot focus on calling, then you should probably stop.

If your script is such a mess that you can't at least use what you have as a guideline, stop. Re-draft your script and start calling again.

There are also times when you might think you should quit, but you should persist. For example, people often think they should stop cold calling when they have a supposedly hot prospect that wants something ASAP.

These "hot" prospects usually turn out to be duds. For example, a client told us he gets telemarketers off the line by interrupting their spiel and telling them, "What a coincidence! We are just about to make a decision on (whatever they're selling). Send me something right away!" Of course, this guy is just blowing smoke.

We also find new telemarketers often want to stop as soon as they have an appointment to prepare for; an appointment they just got by cold calling.

Well, of course you'd rather prepare for an appointment than keep on cold calling! What a dandy excuse to stop! Don't stop. Preparation can wait and you should keep right on calling.

Troubleshooting ~ What's Wrong With This Picture?

Let's say you've been cold calling for a while now. You're doing everything we've told you to do. Things are going pretty well, but then they seem to fall apart. What to do, what to do…

- **You're not connecting with as many live humans:**

  Try calling at a different time of day, especially before 8 AM and after 5 PM. (You may not call consumers before 8 AM.)

  Try calling on a different day of the week. Surprisingly, Monday is often a great day to call.

  If you're calling people in a particular industry: Are there events occurring that might be taking up their time?

- **You're not getting past gatekeepers:**

  Are you engaging their help? You might need to revise your script to be more humble.

  Ask the gatekeepers to tell you what you should do differently.

  Call early and late.

- **Plenty of contacts, not enough appointments (or sales, if you're selling):**

  Make sure you're not jumping over marketing in your calls, even if you are marketing and selling in one call.

  Are you asking questions? Getting permission first? Uncovering needs and interests per each individual? Avoiding assumptive language?

  Are objections throwing you off? Create a cheat sheet for what to say to try to overcome them.

  These might not be the right prospects. Who actually makes decisions about what you're selling? Who controls the budget?

  Ask the contacts for help and suggestions about who else you should talk to. They will often give you the information mentioned above!

- **You're having trouble sounding enthusiastic:**

  You don't want to sound silly (unless that's the natural you), yet you do want a smile in your voice. Forget posting a mirror; you'll be examining possible blemishes or nose hairs instead of focusing on calls.

  Post a picture that makes you smile. A photograph, a funny card; whatever gives you an inner chuckle.

- **Your scripts begin to sound strange or boring or just not right:**

  Keep in mind that you hear yourself say the same thing over and over and over, but it's new to each contact. You might change your tone of voice and inflection to prevent being bored.

  On the other hand, scripts do get stale. Re-draft, including your ad, if necessary.

- **No-one calls you back:**

  This is not "trouble," this is normal!

  You don't leave voicemail because it will get people to call you back.

  You leave voicemail because when you do reach them, they may remember you from your voicemail, which warms-up the call.

- **You can't tell what is wrong:**

  Are you skipping something? This often happens after you've been very successful. You might feel you've got it all down, so you stop writing down scripts, tracking calls, and so on. No problem! Go back to fundamentals and you'll succeed again.

- **You still can't tell what's wrong:**

  Call us, Savage and Greene. We'll give you some free help. See our website for the phone number: www.savageandgreene.com. You might also find the answer in the free advice section on the website.

"Even if you're on the right track, you'll get run over if you just sit there."

Will Rogers, comedian and ex-train engineer.

Go! Go! Go!

We've now covered what you need to succeed with consultative telemarketing. We've also given you some chances to apply this information in practice.

You know how to prevent frustration and make terrific consultative calls.

You know what to expect—the good, the great, and the N.A.P. Now it's up to you, so we'll provide a few checklists for you.

You might also want to jump on over a few pages to the Tele-Selling section.

"Never mistake movement for action."

Hemingway. Who knows what he meant?

Getting Ready Checklist

❏ If you're calling consumers: Check state and national regulations.

❏ Set telemarketing appointments with yourself: Put them in your calendar. Plan out one month, at least. Telemarket at least every two weeks.

Prepare three telemarketing scripts:

❏ Gatekeepers
❏ Contacts
❏ Voicemail

❏ Test-drive scripts on a friend or co-worker: Does it sound like the real, relaxed you? Revise until each script sounds right.

❏ Pick a call objective: Focus on marketing—the first step of your marketing and sales process. Write the objective on the tracking sheet. Make sure you use words based in reality.

❏ Match one call list to the above objective.

❏ Choose a Dials goal. Write it on the tracking sheet.

❏ Choose a reward. Write it on the tracking sheet.

❏ Clear your calling space. Have all three scripts handy, the one matching your objective most easily seen.

Cold Calling Checklist

❑ Set a timer to remind yourself not to call more than 45 minutes to one hour at a time.

❑ Dial!

❑ Mark off calls as you make them.

❑ Keep calling until you've reached your goal or time limit. (Don't take calls or start another project.)

❑ When you've reached your goal, STOP.

❑ Take your reward!

❑ Put your tracking sheets into a file so you can calculate your business' averages.

❑ Complete any follow-up actions; such as put things into the mail.

❑ Sit back and enjoy success!

The Secrets of Tele-Selling

There are lots of products and services that can be both marketed and sold on the phone. Sometimes all you need is one conversation to close a deal!

This sections covers the wonders of tele-selling.

"The scientific theory I like best is that the rings of Saturn are composed entirely of lost airline luggage."

Mark Russell. He's not that famous, but makes a good argument for selling on the phone.

Hold on There, Bucko!

If you're making outbound calls, you should always take things one step at a time. No matter what you're selling, you still have to market before you move into selling. This means you either need one script that covers both marketing and selling, or two separate scripts. Here are tips for choosing:

> Evel Knievel,
> you're not!
> No jumping to
> sales allowed.

- If you are marketing <u>and</u> selling in <u>one</u> call, you only need one script.

  Your objective is to uncover a good fit and sell to it when you find it.

- If you are marketing and asking for a separate phone appointment (for selling), you should use two scripts.

  Your objective for the marketing script is to qualify on a surface level, and ask for appointments when appropriate.

  Your objective for the selling script is to uncover wants, needs and interests and sell to those.

  Having two scripts helps you focus.

💣 Whether you need one script or two, do not skip marketing. It won't work!

You Know This Stuff Already

Selling on the phone is not much different from selling in person. You must:

- Uncover wants, needs, interests, etc.
- Engage prospects in the process.
- Present to wants, needs, interests, as per each individual prospect.
- Overcome objections.
- Ask for the business.

You must also qualify prospects and manage the sales process accordingly. In addition to uncovering what they might need, want, etc, you have to find out:

- How badly they want it—where does it fit, on their list of priorities?
- Timing—when might they want to move forward?
- Buyers—who has authority to write the check or use the budget?
- Decision Process—how will they decide and who will be involved?

Uncovering all of this information uses the same complicated process that qualifying in person does. You check their annual report for organizational charts; read up on industry hot buttons; consult your crystal ball; and cross your fingers, right? Wrong!

You ask. You ask questions to get information about all of the qualifying issues. To make sure you do all of this, you should do the same thing whether you're on the phone or not: Write it down.

Use a cheat sheet and/or script out how you'll ask qualifying questions. This helps you have the guts to ask instead of guess.

Ah, Grasshopper, it is Not the Same

The difference between selling on the phone and in person is that you don't have that ole body thing going for ya. This means that…

- Both seller and prospect are more easily distracted.

Wave, if you can see me.

- It's harder to get a sense of a problem, or enthusiasm for what you're selling.

- You can't match body language to increase rapport.

- If you're a visual person, it's harder to get your point across.

Dealing successfully with all of the above is not hard. The techniques for tele-selling smooth over these challenges with ease. In fact, if you want to increase your success in selling in person, sell on the phone for a while!

Here is what to do, with some scripted examples (where we can).

- **Countering distraction:**

Set the stage: What you'd like to have happen or how you'll manage the conversation. Ask the prospect for agreement before proceeding.

"What I'd like to do is spend about thirty minutes with you. I have a handful of questions to ask to find out how we might serve you. I'll present my ideas, of course, and I'll ask you to comment on these ideas. Is there anything else you'd like to accomplish today?"

To keep prospects' attention, check in with them a lot. Ask them to comment often. Give them lots of chances to talk by asking questions. Mention your famous other clients.

"Lots of our clients have trouble reinforcing training on the job. Has this been an issue for you, too?"

Use shorter sentences. If you have to take a breath to get a whole sentence out, you've probably lost their attention already.

Take notes by hand or on computer. (If you are going to keyboard, let the prospect know you'll be doing this because they can hear it.)

Keep the conversation short, about half of what you'd do in person. If your sales process is on the longer side, go step by step. Be sure to tell the prospect you want to do this before you get started.

"We might need to have a few conversations to cover things. How about we check in on time at about 45 minutes in?"

If your prospect really wants to continue the conversation, suggest a three minute break. Just put the phone down and come back in three. And, yes, you should take a break too!

You usually can't tell that the conversation has gone on too long, until it's too late.

- **It's harder to get a sense of a problem, or enthusiasm for what you're selling.**

When you use a good script to guide the call, you free your ability to hear the message in their tone. So check on your instincts and ask! This is part of what makes strong tele-selling skills so awesome in person.

"I have to tell you, I sense a concern brewing on that end of the line. Am I right?"

"I'd like to check in: On a scale of 1 to 10, 10 being let's sign a contract right now, how does this sound so far?"

- **You can't match body language to increase rapport.**

You <u>can</u> match a person's tone of voice and use of words to increase a sense of rapport. Don't worry about developing this skill if you're a beginner. It's not crucial to success.

Anyway, building rapport is often misunderstood. Rapport is not about sharing a passion for golf or praising their kiddo's artwork. Rapport is about how you'll work together in the business context.

- **If you're a visual person, it's harder to get your point across.**

Tough! (Just kidding.)

Script out what you want to ask and say. Have these scripts in front of you to satisfy that visual nature of yours.

Look into information-sharing and virtual-meeting applications for the internet. You can not only ask prospects to look at your website or presentation, you can see what they are looking at.

If you want to try to appeal to your prospects' visual sense and want to go low tech, send them something to look at in advance.

Isn't There More to it Than That?

Nope, selling on the phone is pretty darn easy—especially when you practice it a lot.

If you need more about selling, in general, surf on over to the company website, www.savageandgreene.com, for all kinds of free advice.

And now that you've read through this whole book, penciled out exercises, and called your favorite Aunt to tell her how thrilled you are about it, you're ready! Get your P.I.G. in gear and happy telemarketing and tele-selling!

☞ Persistence. Integrity. Guts.®

"I do most of my writing sitting down. That's where I shine."

Robert Benchley, famous author from
the same period in which pants that got shiny went out of fashion.

Selling for the Good Witch

When Dorothy arrived in Oz, the first person she met (not the first person she squished, mind you) was Glinda.

Glinda asked Dorothy, "Are you a good witch, or a bad witch?"

Dorothy replied, "But, I'm not a witch at all!"

If you're raising funds or support for a non-profit agency, charity, or event, you might feel the same way. "But, I'm not a salesperson at all!"

Well, don't freak out on us now… you really are selling something. In this section we teach you how to use good marketing and sales practices in your special arena, including how to create great scripts.

Attention: Skipper-a-headers: Almost all of this book has important information for you and we're not just saying that because we wrote it.

"The first Rotarian was the first man
to call John the Baptist 'Jack.' "

H. L. Mencken, not-famous author apparently familiar with Rotary Clubs.

What Are You Selling?

The first thing you should get clear on is this: What are you selling? What do you offer to your "customers"?

What you're selling is a good feeling. You give your customers (supporters and contributors) a way to feel good about helping make a difference in some way.

> "Professor, where are the instruments!?"

You're selling feeling good about everything from helping National Public Radio, to supporting the Girl Scouts, to enabling legislation, to supporting a local police department, to feeding the last free Pandas.

The range of the kinds of support you might prospect for is huge. Money-wise, it can go from $20, to a commitment to give $2 million (and more, of course).

And you're not always after money! Maybe you're asking local businesses to donate stuff; anything from a box of balloons, to thousands of dollars in printing services.

Or, maybe you're asking people to donate their time. Perhaps you're looking for bachelors to auction-off, or people with cars willing to deliver meals to shut-ins.

Who Are Your "Customers"?

You might think your customers are the people, places or things your cause helps. Not so.

Your customers are those who donate to your cause.

Based on the range of money, stuff, and activities you might ask people to give, the only for-sure thing we can tell you is that your qualified customers are:

(A) Interested in supporting the cause you're calling about.

(B) Ready and able to give what you're asking for.

Prospecting

Just like if you're selling vacuum cleaners, not all prospects will buy what you're selling. Even when prospects support your cause, they might not buy.

When we hold workshops for volunteer tele-funding groups, we often find they have a lot of trouble with this concept. Most volunteers give their time and effort because they feel strongly about the cause. It's hard for them to accept that "able to give" does not always equal "willing to give."

If you find yourself feeling the same way, you're going to create trouble for yourself. You will probably get pretty frustrated and you may scare away donors without realizing it.

The best way to prevent this is to think of telemarketing for a cause as if you were indeed selling vacuum cleaners:

☞ You're looking for a fit between what you have to offer and what prospects want to give.

There will be times when you have N.A.P. (Not a Prospect). There will be people who can't afford it or don't think they can; people who gave at the office; people who don't want to support the cause; people who think you're trying to scam them; and people who don't even want to talk with you at all.

You'll encounter plenty of objections, concerns, etc. when you're calling for the Good Witch. If you're a pro, you'll probably work on overcoming objections. If you're not a pro, then it's usually best to let go without a struggle to preserve your energy.

Scripting for Good Witches

The script for calling for a cause includes:

☎ Who you are and where you're calling from.
Why you're calling.
Ask permission to proceed.
Describe cause and good works.
Ask for support.

Who You Are, etc.

Again, you might not want to use your whole name when you say who you are.

In addition, it might not make sense to say where you're calling from. It often makes more sense to say you're calling on behalf of something (or someone).

"My name is Lesley. I'm calling on behalf of the San Pablo Police League."

Lots of causes have long names and you want to avoid really long where-I'm-calling-from sentences. For example, you don't want to say anything like, *"I'm calling on behalf of the San Pablo Police Wednesday After-School Program Preservation League."*

If your cause has a really long name, work on shortening it. Remember, you'll have a chance to describe the whole deal in just a second!

Why You're Calling

Remember when we said this is the hardest part for regular telemarketing? Same goes for this situation. You want to be very direct about the reason for your call, unlike these guys…

"I'm just calling to thank you for your support."

Yea, sure. You're welcome. Bye!

"I'm calling because you've been such a terrific supporter over the years."

Translation: Because I'll think you'll help again.

"I'm calling because I know you want to save.. ."

Well, since the entire planet seems to be falling apart, you'll have to get in line.

"I'm calling to alert you to a terrible situation in…"

Again with the education; like I'm not reading the papers or watching TV?

But We Do Want Them to Know...

Well, yes, you do want them to know their past support is appreciated—*and what else?*

And you do figure they'll want to help? *Well, that's assumptive.*

And you may indeed feel a need to educate prospects—and, again, *what else do you want to do?*

Let's put you out of your misery: Chances are very good that you want two or three things to happen:

- You want to thank them,.
- You want to give them information.
- And you want to ask for their support.

So, just like with most telemarketing scripts, you need to tell them you'd like two (or three) things to happen, right up-front.

And, even though you're not marketing or selling vacuum cleaners, you want to receive permission before proceeding.

Why I'm Calling Examples for Good Witches

Here are a few examples of the first part of scripting for you, including the part where you ask permission to proceed:

☎ *"Hi, my name is Charlie. I'm calling on behalf of Project Open Hand. I'd like to tell you a bit about the good work Project Open Hand is doing, and then see if you're willing to help.*

May I continue?"

☎ *"My name is Joan and I'm calling from the Save the Rainforest Center. We are helping reverse the trend of losing rainforest. I'd like to tell you a little bit about the situation and then ask if you might like to give some support to the Center.*

Is that okay with you?"

☎ *"This is James. I'm looking for donations for a silent auction. May I tell you about the cause we're supporting and find out if you'd like to pitch in?*

Would you be the best person to talk to about this? Is this a good time?"

☎ *"Good evening! My name is Craig and I'm calling from Kids Work. I'd like to do three things, if I may: I'd like to thank you for your support over the past years, tell you what we've accomplished with that support, and see if you're up for helping us again.*

Is that alright?"

Talking it Up

When you receive permission to proceed, it's your turn to shine. You should briefly describe the situation or cause or event, with heavy emphasis on the good parts and what's working well.

Guilt and fear are poor motivators.

Avoid trying to create a sense of urgency or fear about the cause or situation. This doesn't work very well anymore because the more aware we've become of problems, the easier it is to feel overwhelmed. Overwhelmed people often do nothing, they just want you to go away.

If there is a lot of good to tell, you should stop part-way and give the prospect a chance to say he or she has heard enough.

"There's a lot more I could tell you, but do you have the time?"

If they've heard enough—thumbs up or down—they'll tell you.

It's Guts Time!

Once you've described the cause, event, or whatever, it's time to make a specific request for support.

If you're asking for money, you probably won't have to ask specifically for money. Most people will assume that's what you want.

However, if you have an amount or range of money in mind, you should be specific. For example:

"We're selling tickets so kids can attend the circus. You can buy one ticket for $24, or if you're willing to help a whole family attend, that ticket is $75. Would either of those work for you?"

"You can support KQED with a membership of $60, $75 or $120. We also have special gifts for members who opt to have their membership automatically renewed. May I enroll you as a new member?"

The same goes if you're looking for donations of something other than money. For example:

"We'd love to have an item from your shop to add to our silent auction. Is there something you'd be willing to donate?"

"We appreciate any donations you'd care to make, but we're particularly in need of foster homes for the animals. Would you be willing to take in a cat for a few months?"

But, Mr. Wizard, I Don't Want to Cold Call!

Once you have your scripts ready, you should do all the things we described in other sections to prevent frustration and manage for success.

If you're working with volunteers, there are some special things you can do to help them have a good time and succeed.

☎ Take some time to orient their expectations.

Go over the points in the Great Expectations section. Most of that applies across the board and the rest needs only a little tweaking to fit your situation.

☎ If possible, have them create their own scripts, using a good guideline.

If you're giving them a script to use, encourage them to adjust it so they can use their own words.

☎ **Set dials goals and give them the tools to manage their own process.**

Give them their own tracking sheet.

You might want to present the goal as a group goal. Each caller makes twenty dials for a fabulous total of ___.

Use a timer to make sure they don't call any longer than one hour. 45 minutes would be the best time frame. Make sure they take a break before starting to call again.

☎ **Definitely have a reward and make them take it.**

If you have a group goal, then you might all enjoy your reward as a group, too.

☎ You might also have awards for various things; such as most calls, most formerly-shy, most donations, most helpful, etc.

We Do Freebies

We believe the above will help callers tremendously. We're also happy to pitch in with help on scripting, and on-site training if you're local. If we can be of service, give us a call!

"When I use a word," Humpty Dumpty said
in rather a scornful tone, "it means just what I choose
it to mean—neither more nor less."

Lewis Carroll, possibly using the guise of an innocent egg character
to send a message to his editor.

Your job is not to overcome *every* obstacle
that comes your way.
Your job is to work with every *opportunity*
that comes your way.

If at first you don't succeed, try, try again.
If you still don't succeed, don't be
a darn fool—try something else!
(Mark Twain)

Someone who won't talk with you at all
is not a good challenge,
they're NAP—not a prospect!

For a neat color copy of these inspiring words of wisdom,
contact us and ask for one. It's free!

Elements of Successful Calls

☎ **When calling Gatekeepers:**

Who you are.
Why you're calling.
Ask for help and/or request to proceed.
Description of likely contacts, just in case.
Thank you.

☎ **When calling contacts/prospects:**

Who you are.
Ad (optional).
Why you're calling.
Request to proceed.
Information sharing, including qualifying prospects.
Check-in, or request to go to next step.

☎ **Voicemail:**

Who you are.
Ad.
Why you're calling.
Call to action.
Your next step.
Who you are again, and how to reach you.

☎ **Calling for the Good Witch:**

Who you are (and on whose or what's behalf).
Why you're calling.
Ask permission to proceed.
Describe cause and good works.
Ask for support.

Sample Tracking Sheet

Date: _____   Time: _____   Calling on list: _____   Objective: _____

Dials Goal: _____   Reward: _____

Dials	Voicemail	Connect	Next Step	NAP
1 2 3 4 5 6 7 8 9 10	1 2 3 4 5 6 7 8 9 10	1 2 3 4 5 6 7 8 9 10	1 2 3 4 5 6 7 8 9 10	1 2 3 4 5 6 7 8 9 10
1 2 3 4 5 6 7 8 9 20	1 2 3 4 5 6 7 8 9 20	1 2 3 4 5 6 7 8 9 20	1 2 3 4 5 6 7 8 9 20	1 2 3 4 5 6 7 8 9 20
1 2 3 4 5 6 7 8 9 30	1 2 3 4 5 6 7 8 9 30	1 2 3 4 5 6 7 8 9 30	1 2 3 4 5 6 7 8 9 30	1 2 3 4 5 6 7 8 9 30
1 2 3 4 5 6 7 8 9 40	1 2 3 4 5 6 7 8 9 40	1 2 3 4 5 6 7 8 9 40	1 2 3 4 5 6 7 8 9 40	1 2 3 4 5 6 7 8 9 40
1 2 3 4 5 6 7 8 9 50	1 2 3 4 5 6 7 8 9 50	1 2 3 4 5 6 7 8 9 50	1 2 3 4 5 6 7 8 9 50	1 2 3 4 5 6 7 8 9 50
	% of Dials	% of Dials	% of Dials	% of Dials

NOTES:

Using the Tracking Sheet

- Use one tracking sheet per objective and calling session.
- Complete all the fields above the table. Include the day of the week in the date field.
- Note what sort of list you're using, to help evaluate the list's value.

- As you call, mark off a number in the dials column, then a number in whatever other column applies. This means you always check off a number in at least two columns.

- Every time the call furthers the marketing/selling process, check one off in the "Next Step" column. For example: If your objective is to request appointments, check one off in this column every time you get an appointment.

- If you're making voicemail calls (planning on getting voicemail) then you might just use the dials column.

- The NAP column includes: Wrong numbers, fax screeches, language barriers, the rare and few people who just won't talk with you at all, and contacts that don't fit your market at all. Do not mark in "NAP" if you plan to call again.

- There is a notes space at the bottom of the sheet. Using a larger piece of paper, you'll have plenty of room to write stuff down. Be sure to note contacts that don't fit your market, in case you want to remove them from your calling list.

- Keep tracking sheets. Use them to pinpoint any problems and create your own success calculation (use the % of Dials areas to do this). Track your success every month to every three months, depending on how often you're telemarketing.

Contact Savage and Greene for a full-size copy of the tracking sheet, or feel free to copy this one.

Other Cool Resources

  For the latest regulations on cold calling:

Do a search for "telemarketing" and "do not call" laws on the internet. Laws vary by state!

For more on marketing:

Guerilla Marketing, Jay Conrad Levinson.

For more about the inside scoop on how our brains work:

Emotional Intelligence, by Daniel Goleman.
Mind Wide Open, by Steven Johnson.

For help with very complex selling cycles:

Strategic Selling, by Robert Miller.

To figure out how to prevent or fix the most common sales performance problems:

Our serious fun "Sales Repair Kit" on CD.
See www.savageandgreene.com or Amazon.com.

For free advice and hot tips on selling:

Again with the www.savageandgreene.com. You can sign up for free monthly sales tips, delivered via email, on our website, too.

Training

This book translates a good deal of what goes on in our "Root Canal" workshop into written word. What's missing is the wonderful human interaction. To bridge this gap, **we offer free coaching with purchase of this book**. Just call to request it!

And, of course, you can engage us to deliver training. In addition to teaching the art of consultative cold calling, we offer programs that cover the entire consultative sales process:

- ☑ From handling fundamentals; such as identifying and expressing benefits;

- ☑ To handling both obvious and hidden objections;

- ☑ To managing long-term business relationships.

We also offer customer service skills training, including teaching service reps to be proactive sellers.

Please see www.savageandgreene.com for program descriptions.

What Makes Us Special

Our training uses dynamic, highly-interactive processes that drive realistic application of concepts. In non-consultant-eze: We work training participants' rear-ends off with practice, practice, practice, so they leave training with actual skills!

Our trainers are experienced sales and service reps, themselves. The practical experience means we can trouble-shoot on the spot.

We embed coaching skills in every training class, so you have the means to reap the full rewards of your investment. (We give you proven tools for training 'reinforcement.')

Not a Big Company?

We're happy to deliver training for groups of people who don't all necessarily work for the same outfit (e.g., Chambers of Commerce, Rotary, and other professional associations).

👍 The same goes for non-profits.

More Coaching

We also offer coaching services to help you overcome any sales challenge you may have. Coaching takes place on the phone (makes sense, eh?). You don't have to sign up for any long term coaching deal, either.

🖱 For more information about any of these options, surf on over to www.savageandgreene.com.

Speak!

Looking for a fabulous speaker? Shawn Greene is available to talk on sales and service performance. Topics include:

- The Art of Consultative Cold Calling.
- Handling Hidden Objections.
- Sales, for Reluctant Sellers.
- The Sales Repair Kit: How to prevent and fix the most common sales problems.

About the Author...

Shawn Greene has taught thousands of people how to cold call successfully—even those who'd rather have a root canal.

Shawn acquired her sales experience in a variety of industries. She's faced the same challenges you may face, and overcame them. No mere theory here!

After years of performing at the top of the sales game, Shawn moved into training. Her clients dig the experience, practical approach, and humor she brings to the table. This book translates that magic into a self-study tool.

Shawn Greene is the fearless leader of Savage and Greene, as well as a dynamic speaker.

About Savage and Greene...

Savage and Greene teaches Persistence, Integrity, Guts® so you get outstanding sales and customer service performance.

Our specialty is teaching sales and customer service on the phone. Programs cover the entire range of selling and service skills. Train-the-trainer is available. For free advice and information about Savage and Greene's services and products, see our cool website www.SavageandGreene.com.

Free Coaching!

Buy this book (or get it as a gift) and you get a free hour of coaching. We're not kidding! Really! It is absolutely free!

Being trainers at heart, we love to help you apply the words of wisdom contained herein.

So email us to arrange your free session! Coach@savageandgreene.com